2008

Best Wi...

True Gifts™ Publishing
Belmont, Massachusetts

We are donating copies of this book
to educational and leadership
institutions around the country.
If you would like to contribute to the
effort, please contact us online at
truegifts.net.

ISBN 13: 978-0-9796701-0-7
ISBN 10:   0-9796701-0-7

A LEADER BECOMES A LEADER

INSPIRATIONAL STORIES OF LEADERSHIP FOR A NEW GENERATION

BY J. KEVIN SHEEHAN

True Gifts™ Publishing

This book was made possible by the lives of the extraordinary people depicted in it.

I owe a debt of personal gratitude to certain friends and individuals who possess the kind of strength and character that I worked to capture here.

I could not have written this book without my wife, Kathy, and my son, Dillon, who have helped me to see the world with fresh eyes. I have been graced with a loving family and a nurturing place in the world, and I cannot thank them enough.

Jan Lindy Boyce has left her distinct and distinguished mark on every page of this book as its designer. Her goodness tinkles the coffee cups on the shelves of life in ways that are hard to describe. I thank her as you can only thank a true creative partner.

Luke O'Neill, who founded the Shackleton School, Cynthia Dickens and Madueno Cabral at Judge Connelly Youth Center, Kathy McKenna at Haley House, Betsy Siggins at Passim Cultural Center, Jatin Desai at the Prashanthi Center, and Sanga Kugabalasooriar live the kinds of lives that are featured in this book, and that serve to make people's lives better. They have been inspirations to me throughout the experience of the research and the writing, and I thank them for their presence.

My friends Joe Thibert, Madelyn Yucht, John Hudson, Ralph Jaccodine, Joe Nevin, Joe Zelloe, Susanne Goldstein, Peter Donaldson, Witt Farquhar, Bertrand Laurence, Jay and Meryle Borden, Rick Cleary, Keith and Priscilla Brailsford, and John Martin-Joy have provided me insight, resilience, and soul at some of the important turning points in my life in the past several years as this book became a reality. Without them, my life would not have had the kind of resonance necessary to sustain such a vision.

Margo and Don Koten, and Susan and Jeff Sofka, have provided us stability and grace since 1997, when we became a family.

My parents, Jean and Jack, and my sisters, Kathleen and Kelly, have sought to lead lives of meaning since I can remember. It is hard to measure the kind of impact that has had.

Edouard Lock is an ongoing source of inspiration for me.

Nancy Traversy at Barefoot Books, Catherine Drayton at Arthur Pine Associates, Mike Walsh, and Debbie Sandford helped shed light on the complex world of publishing early on, when I was just getting my footing, and I thank them for their gracious insights and support.

Michael Whitaker, Laura DiStasi, and Tracee Dolan have been my right and left hands in organizing this material over the past several years. Loren Gary at the Kennedy School got us to the finish line, and we are grateful for his unusual talent. Sriram Ramgopal and Marcos Solorzano are spirited friends who have brought the book to life on the web.

My colleagues on Huron Avenue have made ten thousand inroads home. Let me thank them for their friendship and camaraderie these years.

Very special thanks to Marian Wright Edelman, Millard Fuller, Elie Wiesel, Anne Lang, Dan Nicolleta, and Aaron Schmidt for their support and guidance in sourcing the photographs in this book.

Carter Caldwell acted as the book's editor, and has been my close friend for many, many years. I am grateful to have a man of such integrity and critical insight always there at my side through thick and thin when I have needed him most.

Finally, it is hard to express my gratitude to all of the teachers over the years who helped me develop the kinds of tools and instincts that have been necessary to capture the lives of these leaders in portrait form. Dr. Paul Piazza, Paul Barrett, the incomparable Ferdinand Ruge, Henri Billet, Bob Brown, Juan Mejia, Jack McCune, Ben DeLoache, Len Schlesinger, Alice Coltrane, Harold Popp, and Bill Scott were some of those teachers, mentors, and guides who helped prepare me for setting out on a long journey such as this. I thought of them often as the night sky's color would some times disappear completely.

Only by passing on our collective wisdom do we evolve as people.

For my beautiful wife, Kathy,
a woman of grace, generosity,
wisdom, and kindness.

For our son, Dillon,
who is my source and my guide.

And for my parents, Jean and Jack,
whose collective heart and soul
informed the making
of this book.

"I learned this, at least, by my experiment:
that if one advances confidently in the direction
of his dreams, and endeavors to live the life which he has
imagined, he will meet with a success unexpected in
common hours. He will put some things behind,
will pass an invisible boundary...
[And] he will live with the license
of a higher order of beings. In proportion
as he simplifies his life, the laws of the universe
will appear less complex, and solitude
will not be solitude, nor poverty poverty,
nor weakness weakness.

If you have built castles in the air,
your work need not be lost;
that is where they should be.
Now put foundations under them."

—HENRY DAVID THOREAU
Walden

virtues OF LEADERSHIP

A LEADER BECOMES A LEADER

virtues OF LEADERSHIP
continued

TABLE OF contents

We have all been moved at some point in our lives by great leadership. It is as organic a part of the human landscape as a sudden waterfall or the deep mystery of a majestic canyon is in nature. You often don't know that it's coming. You will never forget its impact.

We created this collection of stories about the development of great leaders to commemorate and celebrate the moments that have moved and inspired people around the world.

Mother Teresa, who moved many people as a leader, sometimes quite literally off the streets of Calcutta, said once, "You can never do great things. You can only do small things with great love."

I could hear her words resonate in these pages again and again as I worked to capture the stories of these celebrated leaders. Inspired leadership, it seems, is not about big things. In fact, it turns out that the leaders featured here often found greatness in the smallest things, in the essential human stuff such as discipline, patience, truth, compassion, creativity, and fairness.

Leadership comes in both the public arena and in more private moments where one mind, one heart, one spirit meets another through timeless art and literature. Leadership also happens through simple example, such as when a great athlete, by sheer human excellence, demonstrates for a global village what is possible.

To capture leaders' stories is to record their inner triumphs: Abraham Lincoln rising from desperate poverty to educate himself and become the grand statesman that he was; Mohandas Gandhi suffering the indignities and humiliations of an oppressive society to become a visionary leader who found the potential for greatness in every person he worked to set free.

Leaders come from places as varied as Skopje, Macedonia, and Hardin County, Kentucky, and from disciplines as different as marine biology and freedom fighting. They come, and they touch our lives. They change the way we work, live, and see the world.

The leaders featured in this book cleared paths in a wood and marked them, so that we could wander those trails again and again to wonder outside ourselves. Their stories light the paths with colors and sounds that we can still see and hear, if we look and listen closely enough.

Each of these lives was in some way a message. Each of these lives remains a part of our collective trail map.

I have been humbled to do the research and writing. I hope you enjoy these stories.

J. KEVIN SHEEHAN

CHAPTER 1

A LEADER BECOMES A LEADER
IN TIME

"In an imperfect work, time is an ingredient,
but into a perfect work, time does not enter."

–HENRY DAVID THOREAU
author, philosopher, and naturalist

A LEADER BECOMES A LEADER
IN TIME

He borrowed a horse and wagon in 1889 and wandered off into the wilderness around Concord, Massachusetts, to a site on Walden Pond, where he had built a small cabin to live in. He carried with him a small package of personal items, including pen and paper. There, over the course of a twenty-six-month experiment in living alone with the essential things, he would, in concert with the magnificence of the natural beauty around him, change the lives of generations of readers. There, Henry David Thoreau wrote his famous *Walden* essays, which would profoundly affect some of the most influential leaders of the next century–people as diverse as Mohandas Gandhi, Dr. Martin Luther King, Jr., and Nelson Mandela–through the force of his spirit and the power of his pen.

"I went to the woods because I wished to live deliberately," Thoreau wrote, "to front only the essential facts of life, and see if I could not learn what it had to teach." Thoreau's adventure was that of a leader: his was a solitary quest into an open wilderness of change, danger, potential, and deep, abiding mystery. His work on Walden Pond elevated a society by envisioning a promised place that has carried generations of followers to a similar freedom and new-found awareness ever since.

Thoreau developed in himself an energy and attitude that has shaped the philosophy and actions of some of the most consequential leaders of the twentieth century. Mohandas Gandhi, India's freedom fighter who liberated in his work over a billion people on two continents, modeled his philosophy of civil disobedience and nonviolence after that of Thoreau. César Chávez, Rachel Carson, and Frank Lloyd Wright, three of the twentieth century's preeminent leaders and innovators, integrated Thoreau's teachings as an important element in their own philosophies.

"In an imperfect work, time is an ingredient," Henry David wrote, "but into a perfect work, time does not enter." For Thoreau, a spirit exists in work of a high order that operates outside of time to touch readers and listeners whenever they prove ready.

Abraham Lincoln, Frank Lloyd Wright, and John Coltrane made themselves into powerful leaders by forging their own characters in alliance with the best qualities of humankind's relationship with time–persistence, grace, intensity, and endurance. Lincoln's exceptional capacity for persistence manifested itself during the seemingly endless days of the American Civil War, when the task required a leader who could persevere until the Declaration of Independence's core tenet that "all men are created equal" could find a foothold in every corner of the country. Frank Lloyd Wright believed that beauty was an absolute quality, and he imbued his life with a simple dedication to finding that essence in the world of architecture and the natural world around him.

Leaders whose work we remember as timeless dedicate themselves to works of a higher order–work that magnifies their natural passions and talents, work that connects them to a commitment to a greater good. They develop in themselves an ability to see beyond time's edges, to a place where transcendent truths and ends subsume all the intermittent failures and frictions of our days.

You can reexperience this dedication in the legacy of Thoreau's essays. You can reexperience it in the words of President Lincoln's Second Inaugural Address, the motion of Frank Lloyd Wright's Fallingwater, and the notes of John Coltrane's *Giant Steps*. You can watch for yourself as their works stop time and live on.

"With malice towards none,
with charity for all … let us strive on to finish the work we are in …
to do all which may achieve and cherish a just and lasting peace
among ourselves and with all nations."

—ABRAHAM LINCOLN
16th president of the United States, from his Second Inaugural Address, inscribed on the Lincoln Memorial

Abraham Lincoln became a leader over time,
weathering the worst circumstances to carry a nation to higher ground.

IN TIME

If you had read his résumé just before he became President, you might not have hired him. He had moved around a lot early in life, from profession to profession. Although he had great success as a lawyer and some success as a legislator, his professional career had more losses in it than it did victories. And the losses were pretty impressive—two businesses and eight elections. His only leadership experience had been as a Congressman in the United States House of Representatives. But his fierce competence as an attorney, his towering moral stature, and a piercing political vision made him a force to be reckoned with. These qualities would win him the White House in 1860. During his first term, the bold, young political experiment that was the United States of America would be on the verge of complete collapse. It would be his to save or lose.

HIS PERSISTENCE WAS THE STUFF OF LEGEND

Abraham Lincoln had not become the 16th president of the United States to lose the union that he held so dear. He recognized the historic moment for what it was, and battled back against the forces of anarchy that were threatening the country's survival with every talent he possessed and in every moment that would be his. In the face of what seemed insurmountable conflict, he wrote with the power of Jefferson, stood with the force of Washington, and thought with the precision of Franklin. His persistence was legendary, powered by a faith in the strength of people to sustain themselves through the worst crises and circumstances. He weathered depression, a near-fatal disease, and financial debt that weighed on him most of his adult life. During his presidency, he endured vicious personal criticism, which extended to his policies, and even to his wife. His worst adversary would prove to be the chaos and confusion of a young nation pulled apart by countervailing political forces that some said could never be quieted. The South's economy depended on the institution of slavery. Many of the country's founders in the previous century had recognized that such an abhorrent practice had to end.

Lincoln came by his extraordinary perseverance honestly. No other president of the United States rose from such humble beginnings. The cabin he grew up in had a dirt floor. The mattress he used to sleep on as a child was a combination of leaves, twigs, and animal skins. In some ways, the harshest life prepared him for the extraordinary burden he would carry as president, working to enforce the Declaration of Independence's core tenet "that all should have an equal chance."

There are very few leaders in American political history who have captured the human imagination quite like Abraham Lincoln. He led the nation through the moral, economic, and military crisis that nearly destroyed what the country's founders had created in 1776. He held that union of diverse states together in its greatest moment of crisis. By sheer force of discipline and will, he carried the nation on his shoulders. On the strength of his magnificent words, he led the country out of the devastation of slavery and through the Civil War, which caused brother to kill brother and families to come apart. In all, 620,000 people died.

At the Lincoln Memorial, inscribed in the walls of stone, some of his most famous words carry the spirit and legacy of this man to the next generations. "With malice towards none, with charity for all, with firmness in the right as God gives us to see the right, let us strive on to finish the work we are in; to bind up the nation's wounds, to care for him who shall have borne the battle and for his widow and his orphan, to do all which may achieve and cherish a just and lasting peace among ourselves and with all nations."

ABE'S LIFE

1809
Abraham Lincoln is born to Thomas and Nancy Hanks Lincoln in a log cabin in Hardin County, Kentucky.

1817
Young Abe becomes a great lover of books, and enjoys hearing stories of the outside world from friends of the family who come to visit and talk on the front porch into the night.

1818
Abe's beloved mother dies of milk sickness at the age of thirty-four, leaving him deeply bereaved.

1831
At twenty-two, Lincoln leaves home to put down roots as an adult in the small village of New Salem, Illinois. He has had one year's formal education.

1831-1840
Early in his career, Abe opens a store. He later works at a variety of jobs that include postman, soldier, and surveyor. He becomes a self-taught attorney and is eventually elected to the local legislature, where he will serve four terms.

1840
Lincoln falls in love with Mary Todd, the daughter of a prominent local banker. She agrees to marry him.

1846
Lincoln is elected to the U.S. House of Representatives. After two trying years, during which he is unable to advance legislation, he returns to Springfield, Illinois, defeated and doubtful of his political future.

1850s
Lincoln becomes one of the most successful lawyers in the state of Illinois.

1854
Congressman Stephen Douglas champions legislation in Congress to allow the institution of slavery to extend to two new western territories, Kansas and Nebraska. Lincoln recognizes an important political opening and denounces the new legislation.

1858
After the famous debates with Douglas during their race for Senate, the propagation of slavery beyond the South becomes the cornerstone issue of the U.S. Presidential contest. Lincoln wins the Republican Party's nomination, and is elected President.

1861-1865
The South secedes from the Union, despite Lincoln's warning in his First Inaugural Address that he will go to any length, including war, to maintain the nation's integrity. The South establishes the Confederate States of America, and the Civil War begins. The war will rage for four years, with 620,000 lives lost and hundreds of thousands severely wounded.

1863
President Lincoln issues the Emancipation Proclamation, freeing some four million slaves.

1865
The Confederacy surrenders at Appomattox on April 9th, bringing the Civil War to an end. Just six days later, President Abraham Lincoln is assassinated at Ford's Theater in Washington, D.C.

GLIMPSES OF YOUTH

Abraham Lincoln's classmates in grammar school recognized in him early on the leadership skills that he would develop more fully later in life.

THE ENDURANCE OF
FRANK LLOYD WRIGHT

"I attend the greatest of all churches.
I put a capital *N* on nature and call it my church."

–FRANK LLOYD WRIGHT
from Ken Burns's PBS documentary, *The Greatest American Architect*

Frank Lloyd Wright became a leader in architecture,
building on the beauty of the most enduring things.

IN TIME

He is regarded by many as the greatest American architect. But in his lifetime, Frank Lloyd Wright's work was ridiculed; his estate was burned to the ground by an aggrieved employee; and he lived from commission check to commission check, on the brink of financial disaster for most of his life. The adversity, at times, was overwhelming. But as an artist who pressed the bounds of great design in such master spaces as the classic residence Fallingwater, in rural Pennsylvania, and his own home, Taliesin, in the Wisconsin River Valley, he was used to such challenges.

HE ALWAYS TOOK THE LONG VIEW

For many decades–from his most prolific period of 1899-1909 to when he died in 1959–he found in the beauty of his work sanctuary from the burdens of his world. He would open himself to the rapture of the creative process, and let that rapture transport him to a place of new art and fresh perspective. In his art, he journeyed to a place of such peace and transcendent vision that the dramatic disruptions around him–many of which he brought on himself–would vanish like a dawn's mist caught in the rays of the early morning sun.

His detractors point to a genius's petulant and impulsive behavior. He was short with people, rebellious, and impatient–as genius can be when the outside world has a hard time keeping pace. He was subject to whim and fancy, often fundamentally altering a project's direction in midstream as his internal creative forces drove him with fresh passion and new ways of thinking and expressing himself. But his point of view was so important, and his body of work so fresh and lasting, that his legacy has changed our collective design landscape with timeless achievements in design and structure. Seventeen of his buildings are National Historic Landmarks.

Fallingwater, his masterwork residence set above a glorious waterfall in western Pennsylvania, embodies the philosophy of the man who made it. Wright explained his creative process when the building was conceived: "There in a beautiful forest was a solid, high rock ledge rising beside a waterfall, and the natural thing seemed to be to cantilever the house from that rock bank over the falling water." He encouraged the owner, his sponsor, to new heights in design: "I want you to live with the waterfall, not just to look at it, but for it to become an integral part of your lives." His spaces "hugged the earth," conspiring with his country's open prairie landscape to provide a newfound sense of freedom, longing, and adventure. He explained how integral his placement of a building could be with typical directness and aplomb: "If you build on top of the hill, you lose the hill."

It was during his teenage years that Wright first encountered the works of Ralph Waldo Emerson and the Transcendentalists. Their fascination with nature as a source of inspiration, enduring value, and ultimate peace gave him a perspective that he never lost. His family's eventual move to industrial Chicago challenged these initial underpinnings with the shock and turbulence of an emerging city. The new industrialization proved to be an adversary of such momentum that abandoning the country ways of life seemed unavoidable. But the visionary student architect saw in the upheaval new forms of beauty, and he integrated the rural American influences of his youth with the modern influences that were flooding Chicago to create quintessentially American architectural spaces that would have no equal.

To be in one of his spaces was to meditate on the grand beauty that was his buildings' natural surroundings. With his attention to detail extending to the furniture and cooking utensils in his spaces, Wright created a world of organic fancy and imagination that was utterly timeless and freeing. It was in his commitment to nature's timeless principles that he would find a lasting place for himself and his art. He took the long view, essentially creating a welcome space for nature in the increasingly enclosed world of humankind.

THE INTENSITY OF
JOHN COLTRANE
1926-1967

"There is never any end. There are always new sounds to imagine."

—JOHN COLTRANE
jazz innovator

John Coltrane became a leader in music
by creating sounds that had never existed.

He set the world of jazz on fire, playing modally across the chords in torrents of notes and sounds like no one who had come before him.

You need only view a photograph of John Coltrane to understand the intensity that was there. There was no moderation in the man, nothing to moderate; in fact, all the elements of John Coltrane seemed aflame. He lifted genius to a new plane, and made the spiritual an integrated part of his compositions. It was a quest to find new music–sounds that had never been made before. He pursued his quest with a gentleman's demeanor and a rogue's passion. You'd watch him there, planted firmly atop his horn, dressed elegantly in a black suit, with a look of awe in his eyes as truths unfolded from the notes that he played. They astonished even the man who had made them.

HE SAID HE WAS CHASING ETERNITY

Nat Hentoff, the influential jazz historian, explained the power and import of Coltrane's musical legacy: "He was instrumental in freeing the concept of what a jazz performance is. Rarely, I think, in any form of music has one man so thoroughly revealed himself."

He started out like many of us, playing clarinet in the town band and honing his skill as part of the high school music program. He went on to refine those skills in the Navy. And then the Trane started to roll.

His overwhelming discipline and drive were evident throughout his career in the most elemental things, including his contracts. By the end of his career, he would demand forty thousand dollars an album, upfront, in 1960s dollars. This was at a time when many musicians were watching their copyrights being taken from them in contractual agreements that were inches thick and often abusive, requiring first-class lawyers to negotiate.

At times in his life, his intensity would veer off track and reduce to obsession. His enduring quest for finding fresh new sounds caused him to sometimes leave the bandstand while other players were soloing, to pursue his own musical journey offstage, where he could still hear the sounds of genius ringing clear. At times, he relieved the pressure of his intense pursuits by imbibing alcohol and drugs, habits that eventually caused Miles Davis to fire him for a time from his famous band. But Coltrane used even the most difficult things, like kicking a drug habit, to push himself, free himself, and move his music higher: He wrote, "[It] led me to a richer, fuller, more productive life. In gratitude, I humbly asked to be given the means and privilege to make others happy through music."

There is a jazz instrumentalist and historian in Washington, D.C., named Andrew White, who has spent much of his career transcribing and recreating the lines of John Coltrane. If you get a chance to see him play Coltrane's music live, you'll notice how physically difficult it is for him to play to the end of his lines. It was so difficult for Coltrane, himself, that people would sometimes give him oxygen to sustain him to the end of a live performance.

Asked why he played so frenetically and so long, to the point of passing out, he responded that he could sense eternity just around the corner and could not stop. He would not stop playing, he said, until he reached that place.

1926
John Coltrane is born September 3rd to John William and Alice Blair Coltrane in Hamlet, North Carolina. His father, a tailor by trade and a musician by hobby, fills the family home with his love of music.

1941-1945
In high school, Coltrane joins the school band, playing first the E-flat alto saxophone, then the clarinet, and, finally, the tenor saxophone.

1945-1955
Coltrane makes his name playing saxophone in Philadelphia R & B bands in the 1940s, and then goes on to play with some of the best jazz innovators, from Thelonius Monk to Dizzy Gillespie, in the 1950s. As his career takes flight, so, too, does his dependence on alcohol and drugs.

1957
Charlie Parker dies of drug addiction in 1955, and, as a result, Coltrane determines that he will end his own addiction to drugs and alcohol cold turkey at his mother's house.

1958
Coltrane joins the Miles Davis Quintet for a second time and new horizons open for his playing. "Miles's music gave me freedom," he said. Davis would add: "Trane was the loudest, fastest saxophonist I've ever heard.... He was possessed when he put that horn in his mouth."

Late 1950s
Coltrane begins to record his own records and to develop a melodic approach that is unlike any that has come before him. He composes pieces like "Naima" that ring with a unique clarity and emotion.

1960-1967
Coltrane forms the John Coltrane Quartet, and unleashes in a prolific seven-year run some of the most innovative and spirited music that jazz has known. Classic albums from the period include *My Favorite Things*, *Giant Steps*, and *A Love Supreme*.

1965
Downbeat magazine names John Coltrane its Jazzman of the Year and *A Love Supreme* its Record of the Year. Coltrane tells *Jazz* magazine: "I want to be a force for real good.... I know that there are bad forces...that bring suffering to others and misery to the world, but I want to be the opposite."

1967
Coltrane dies of liver disease at age forty in Huntington, Long Island. He has been a controversial musician whose rapturous sounds and pioneering directions have bent the jazz medium in important ways that are still being understood.

GLIMPSES OF YOUTH

As a teenager, John Coltrane was very particular about the way his eggs were cooked. His egg needs were so daunting that his aunt and mother finally told him to make them himself.

"Your fellow citizens in various portions of the country have expressed their preference for you as the candidate of the Republican party for the next presidency…. There are those around you, sir, who have watched with mainly interest and pride your upward march from obscurity to distinction. There are those here who know something of the obstacles which have lain in your pathway. Our history is prolific in examples of what may be achieved by ability, perseverance [sic] and integrity…but in the long list of those who have come from the humblest beginnings, won their way worthily to proud distinction, there is not one can take precedence of the name of Abraham Lincoln."

–MILTON HAY
Secretary of State for the United States
from *Abraham Lincoln: A Biography*, by Benjamin P. Thomas

"Beyond question the Imperial Hotel [in Tokyo, Japan] was a monumental example of the Wright genius. To create a total environment, he engaged himself to the fullest in the building's design and construction, from the purchase of a stone quarry to the delineation of chinaware for the dining room. Mr. Wright became the Imperial Hotel… during the nine years of its realization. Beauty and harmony were the qualities he sought in everything–a face, a woman's dress, an arrangement of greens, an oriental sculpted figure, a house on its site, a landscape. …Beauty, to Mr. Wright, was not a matter of taste. It was neither relative nor subject to the fluctuations of history or culture. Beauty was everlasting, an absolute quality existing in a 'realm of essences.'"

–EDGAR TOFEL
apprentice to Frank Lloyd Wright
from *Years with Frank Lloyd Wright: Apprentice to Genius*

IN TIME

"As the rest of the band members started to arrive, [Coltrane] would nod a greeting but never stop playing. He was deep into another world. He set the atmosphere for the sessions, because as the musicians entered the room they would hear where he was coming from and develop an instant 'attitude' for what they should play."

–TOM DOWD
recording engineer for John Coltrane
from *The Heavyweight Champion: John Coltrane, The Complete Atlantic Recordings*

per·se·ver·ance

1.
Steady persistence in
adhering to a course
of action

2.
A belief, or a purpose;
steadfastness

en·dur·ance

1.
The act, quality, or
power of withstanding
hardship or stress

2.
The state or fact of
persevering

3.
Continuing existence;
duration

in·ten·sity

1.
Exceptionally great
concentration, power,
or force

2.
The amount
or degree of strength
of electricity, light,
heat, or sound per unit
area or volume
(in physics)

CHAPTER 2

A LEADER BECOMES A LEADER
WITH VISION

"Some men see things as they are and ask, 'Why?'
I dream things that never were and ask, 'Why not?'"

–ROBERT F. KENNEDY
United States Senator (paraphrasing George Bernard Shaw)

A LEADER BECOMES A LEADER
WITH VISION

When playwright and philosopher George Bernard Shaw wrote, in 1949, "You see things as they are and ask, 'Why?' I dream things as they never were and ask, 'Why not?'" he could not have imagined that these words would ring a generation later from the lips of Robert F. Kennedy to influence people around the world. It is on the mettle of powerful visions and ideas that leaders forge the future.

Dr. Martin Luther King, Jr., in the mid-1950s, stoked the embers left behind by early civil rights protests in places like Montgomery, Alabama, and ignited a flame that would engulf a nation with a new vision of equal rights for citizens everywhere, regardless of their color. Dr. King championed the promise from his nation's constitution to elevate a people. He saw in the divisions of racial prejudice an opportunity to transform a society–from one undermined by great fissures caused by institutionalized repression to one defined by liberty and justice for all.

Mother Teresa saw in the dark streets of death and human misery in Calcutta an opportunity for service, decency, and human healing. She and her fellow Sisters of Charity knelt before the hopeless and the dying in the darkest nights of the most desperate poverty and moved them into safe houses of light, compassion, and medical care. People were allowed to die with dignity under her organization's care. Lying in their beds late at night, many would smile with relief and awe as they realized that their fates had changed so dramatically and so unexpectedly. It didn't matter that they were dying. Simple acts of kindness sent a message to the world that one could make a difference in the most hopeless of circumstances just by lending a hand and doing the right thing. She instilled in the world a consciousness of change–the idea that transformation was possible in ordinary places by ordinary people doing extraordinary things.

Franklin Delano Roosevelt must have seen in the catastrophes of a world at war and international economic collapse in the early years of the twentieth century the potential for a new era–one defined by greater economic justice, stronger international security, and new freedom for countries around the world. He lit a torch of optimism that shone across the oceans, and he did it from a wheelchair that carried his polio-stricken body. He galvanized America's allies with the strength of his very person.

These leaders' ability to look beyond their immediate circumstances and to envision what was possible around the next corner made them invaluable contributors to their times. In the most intractable crises, they found causes that were just, methods that were innovative, and objectives that were noble. They served to unify people in their darkest moments with a common language. The language was one of human principles–justice, hope, and compassion. They moved individuals to a higher ground where leadership, experience, and hard work could triumph over dramatic odds.

"Free at last. Free at last.
Thank God almighty, we are free at last."

–MARTIN LUTHER KING, JR.
civil rights activist

Martin Luther King became a leader in human rights
by dreaming things other people were afraid to dream.

WITH VISION

He didn't intend to change history.

In fact, his first career plan was to finish a graduate degree in divinity, and then return to his hometown to take over his father's church. It was a path that had been preordained by two generations of ministers, his father and grandfather. It was a legacy that was both empowering and welcoming, embracing principles that he loved, and keeping him close to his family's roots.

HIS DREAM CHANGED A NATION

But events and history have a way of beckoning visionary leaders to the front lines.

At just twenty-six years old, he was drafted to lead a civil rights protest march in Montgomery, Alabama. Soon thereafter, he found himself in the crucible of civil unrest, and on the fault line of social change that shook the tectonic plates on which a nation stood. He responded to the call by leading the civil rights movement in the United States with unparalleled vision, charisma, and personal strength. He responded to the call by transforming the call itself. A request to lead a protest march became a journey to the heart of social justice; the call to lead a small gathering became a national civil rights movement of nonviolent resistance.

Rosa Parks said of him, "It seemed as if every time he spoke, he said something I wanted or needed to hear. After we listened to one of his messages, we were empowered to continue. His charisma and appeal continued to move me until his death."

When we idealize him, it is easy to forget that, at the height of his power, he was one of the most hated figures in America. It is easy to forget that the conflicts within the civil rights movement, between advocates of nonviolent resistance and advocates of violent confrontation, were so powerful that he was nearly upended several times in his short career.

But it was in moments such as the march on Washington, in 1963, that King rose above it all. That August, on the steps of the Lincoln Memorial, he expressed a vision of the future that had no second. Dr. King's singular presence that day utterly humanized the oppression and suffering of millions of African-Americans, while sending a refrain to the choruses of history that has riveted generations of listeners who just close their eyes to hear his voice saying it again: "Free at last. Free at last. Thank God almighty, we are free at last."

If you ever wonder about the source of his inspiration, watch the film of the speech closely. Two-thirds of the way in, King leaves his scripted speech and erupts in a gospel improvisation that is one of the great moments in oratorical history. It's human magic. You can see him as he steps off the edge, creating the words and phrases as he goes, rising as if on an ascending mountain stair, from verse to powerful verse. On his words that day, he carries the crowd with him to that mountain top, so that each can see what he has seen.

He has been to the mountain top and is not afraid to die. Reflecting on the momentum of his life, he said that events had transformed him. Maybe so. But he transformed events, and through the power of his spirit, created a vision that has inspired and pressed people forward–towards a better day and that vision–ever since.

MARTIN'S LIFE

1929
Martin Luther King, Jr., is born in Atlanta, Georgia, to Reverend Martin Luther King, Sr., and Alberta Williams King.

1934
The young boy has his first experiences with racial discrimination when neighborhood parents refuse to let their white children play with him.

1953
At twenty-four years old, Martin marries Coretta Scott, a New England Conservatory graduate student studying concert singing and violin, and also a woman of uncommon intellectual and artistic gifts.

1951-1955
King matriculates as a graduate student at the Boston University School of Theology, receiving his doctorate in systematic theology in 1955.

1955
Rosa Parks is arrested for not giving up her seat to a white person on a public bus in Montgomery, Alabama. African-American women in the city organize a boycott of segregated buses, and King joins the protest.

1956
King's house is bombed.

1957
King is instrumental in founding the Southern Christian Leadership Conference, a group created to fight segregation and advance civil rights.

1958
King is nearly killed in Harlem by a crazed female assailant who stabs him in the chest.

1959
King travels to India to study the philosophy of Mohandas Gandhi. He spends time at Gandhi's ashram, and returns to the U.S. with a fuller understanding of Gandhi's philosophy of radical change through nonviolent resistance.

1960-1963
King and the SCLC organize protests and marches to bring basic civil rights to African-Americans. Their work leads to the passage of the Civil Rights Act of 1964, and the Voting Rights Act of 1965.

1963
King makes his historic *I Have a Dream* speech.

1964
King wins the Nobel Peace Prize.

1968
King addresses a joyous crowd of supporters: "We've got some difficult days ahead. It really doesn't matter what happens now, because I've been to the mountaintop.... And I've seen the promised land. I may not get there with you. But I want you to know tonight that we as a people will get to the promised land."

He is assassinated on a motel balcony the next morning.

GLIMPSES OF YOUTH

As a teenager, King participated in an academic competition a couple of hours outside of Atlanta. On a crowded bus, the driver ordered King and his teacher to surrender their seats to two white passengers who had just boarded. King reported after the incident that he had never felt so aggrieved.

"You can never do great things.
You can only do small things with great love."

—MOTHER TERESA
founder of the Sisters of Charity mission

Mother Teresa became a leader by
serving people others were not willing to serve.

WITH VISION

She never wrote her thoughts down, or published a book. She believed that to write things down would have detracted from the power of her work, and from the intimacy of the Sisters of Charity's life with the poor. She left her worldly connections behind at just fourteen years old, believing that a mission beyond the bounds of family and neighborhood was the right place for her.

SHE MADE THE WORLD FAMILY

But the words she spoke in life, reported back to us by contemporaries in service, such as Jose Luis Gonzalez-Baludo, reveal a revolutionary vision of social justice that would set the word around her upside down. "I have come…to realize that it is being unwanted that is the worst disease that any human being can ever experience," she explained.

She founded the Sisters of Charity mission on a simple precept: if you could bring hope, love, and comfort to the worst off and most despairing in their dying hours, then you could bring love and comfort to anyone, anywhere in the world.

And so it was. At the beginning, the sisters moved women and men ravaged by the elements, near death, into hospitals. They stood vigil in those hospital lobbies to verify, and sometimes force, their admission. They comforted the abandoned and forgotten in their last hours, to make sure that they knew at the end someone was there who loved them.

When you consider her actions, and the words she had to share, you know that this woman interpreted the world around her with the eyes of a mystic and the hands of a healer.

Of the poor, she said, "The poor are great! The poor are wonderful! The poor are very generous! They give us much more than what we give them."

She said about peace, "Peace and war begin at home. If we truly want peace in the world, let us begin by loving one another in our own families. If we want to spread joy, we need for every family to have joy."

She said of the developed nations, "In the developed countries, there is a poverty of intimacy, a poverty of spirit, of loneliness, of lack of love. There is no greater sickness in the world today than that one."

And as she saw, she did. She made the world her family, taking her faith at its word and injecting the life she found with love and compassion. She derived her concepts from the man whose shoes she chose to walk in. She derived her success from the way she walked in those shoes–selflessly, deliberately, lovingly, without compromise.

She embraced the idea that the ultimate spirit thrived in the poorest of the poor, and so carried them off the streets with the urgency that her philosophy required.

"Mother Teresa is one of those liberated souls who has transcended all barriers presented by race, religion, and nationality," said the president of the Republic of India. "In our present-day troubled world…the life that is lived and the work that is carried out by people like Mother Teresa bring new hope for the future of mankind."

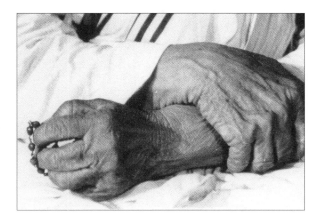

TERESA'S LIFE

1910
Mother Teresa is born Agnes Gonxha Bojaxhid in Skopje, Macedonia.

1910-1917
Agnes grows up in a small family of Albanian descent. Her father is a businessman, a building contractor, and her mother, a seamstress. The family is generous, offering support and guidance to neighborhood families who find themselves in trouble.

1917
Agnes's father is murdered when she is seven.

1922
At twelve years old, she decides that she will join a religious order and make spiritual work her life's undertaking.

1928
She becomes a nun at the age of eighteen, joining a teaching convent in a suburb of Dublin, Ireland.

1929-1946
She serves as a geography, history, and divinity teacher in a Calcutta high school. During her tenure, she learns the local languages, Bengali and Hindi, and rises through the ranks to become principal.

1946
Riding a train in Calcutta, Teresa has a vision that she will leave the convent and work the rest of her life with the city's poor.

1948
Teresa leaves her order to live in the heart of the slums, and tend to the most impoverished and dying in their final hours. Over time, her work evolves to protecting street kids and orphans, housing lepers, and creating hospices for addicts and the homeless.

1950-1990
In 1950, she receives permission to found the Sisters of Charity. Its role of rendering "free service to the poor and the unwanted, irrespective of caste, creed nationality or race" leads to the creation of programs for the unwanted and impoverished in ninety countries around the world.

1979
Mother Teresa receives the Nobel Peace Prize. Professor John Sanness, the chairman of the Norwegian Nobel committee, says of her: "Mother Teresa has personally succeeded in bridging the gulf that exists between the rich nations and the poor nations. Her view of the dignity of man has built a bridge."

1997
Mother Teresa dies of a chronic heart condition that she has struggled with for fifteen years. She had said of her order's work with the poor that it was "a humble service. We try to remain right down on the ground." She worked on the ground to the end, and believed that she had always been the true recipient, able to spend her life in the presence of the poor's hope, generosity, and kindness.

GLIMPSES OF YOUTH

Mother Teresa became a nun at just twelve years old. She had close relationships with her family, but never talked about her childhood later in life, believing that that would detract from the power of the spiritual work.

"Take any method and try it.
If it fails, admit it frankly and try another, but above all, try something."

—FRANKLIN DELANO ROOSEVELT
32nd president of the United States

Franklin Roosevelt became a leader during the Great Depression,
lifting the nation with his extraordinary capacity for hope and optimism.

WITH VISION

It is hard to imagine what the world would have become without his vision and ability to lead people. The 32nd president of the United States, Franklin Delano Roosevelt, spent twelve turbulent years in the White House, guiding his nation through the twentieth century's two greatest crises. First, the Great Depression threatened every corner of the world's economy. In the United States alone, a half-million homeowners were forced to default on their mortgages, fifty percent of the urban population was out of work, crops rotted on farms across the country, and banks and capital markets collapsed. Then, the catastrophic second world war set the world on fire in an inferno of mass destruction unlike anything the world had ever seen. It was ignited by the maniacal ambition and hateful philosophy of one man–Adolf Hitler. The days of evil that would be the twelve years of Hitler's reign left sixty million people dead worldwide in the worst military conflagration in recorded history.

HIS OPTIMISM LIFTED NATIONS

He faced each crisis with an extraordinary faith that things would work out. He was able to transmit that confidence to a country and people beleaguered, at times crushed, by the overwhelming odds. His vision was simple: we will find a solution or make one. He exuded such steadfast vision, calm, and optimism that he was able to lift his nation by the strength of his persona. Winston Churchill, Britain's prime minister and his longtime political ally and close personal friend, said that meeting him was like opening a bottle of champagne. The easy confidence that he radiated, fedora tipped rakishly to one side, caused friends and foes alike to revere his innate capacities as he worked with the allies to battle against the horrors that roared like endless thunder through the world's darkened skies. Isaiah Berlin, the British philosopher, said of him, "Peoples far beyond the frontiers of the U.S. rightly looked to him as the most genuine and unswerving spokesman of democracy."

It didn't come easy. The vast structure of social reforms that he put in place, called the New Deal, shielded common people from the sharpest edges of an emerging capitalist system. The changes created hatred of him in the establishment, which preferred things status quo. His battle with polio left his energy depleted, his body semi-mobile, and his spirit scarred after a seven-year struggle. He had an abundant cache of character flaws, from deviousness and ruthlessness to being manipulative, vengeful, dissembling, and underhanded in the pursuit of his political ends. But through his bout with polio, he developed a profound compassion for the common man's struggle with helplessness in the face of the Great Depression. He said at his second inaugural, "The test of our progress is not whether we add more to the abundance of those who have much, it is whether we provide enough for those who have too little." A vast middle class emerged out of Roosevelt's vision for a more balanced economy and social order.

It is hard to understate his majestic capacity for communicating through the dense fog of calamity, desperation, and fear. Millions listened to his weekly radio fireside chats. It was as if he had trekked across the country, going door-to-door: his voice, broadcast live, lit a fire of confidence and hope in the hearth of every living room that was tuned in. Saul Bellow, the celebrated novelist, described experiencing Roosevelt's extraordinary ability to lift his countrymen one hot summer night in Chicago: "Drivers had pulled over, parking bumper to bumper, and turned on the radio to hear Roosevelt. They had rolled down the windows and opened the car doors. Everywhere the same voice. You could follow without missing a single word as you strolled by." The celebrated historian Doris Kearns Goodwin described the effect Roosevelt's life had on his nation: "A great transference of power took place between him and the people. In the early days, the country was fragile, weak, and isolationist, while [Roosevelt] was full of energy, vital, and productive. But gradually, as the President animated his countrymen with his strength and confidence, the people grew stronger and stronger, while he grew weaker and weaker, until in the end, he was so weakened, he died, but the country emerged more powerful, more productive and more socially just than ever before."

1882
Franklin Delano Roosevelt is born to James and Sara Delano Roosevelt on an estate near Hyde Park, New York. His is a childhood lived in a rarefied, stately existence, surrounded by the beauty and grace of New York State's rolling hills.

1887-1896
The young child, an only son, is homeschooled, and learns to speak French, Spanish, and German. He becomes an avid sailor in his youth, and then a strapping sportsman as a teenager.

1905
Roosevelt marries his third cousin, Eleanor, setting the stage for a powerful, lifelong partnership that will have far-reaching political and historic consequences.

1913
Franklin Roosevelt becomes Assistant Secretary of the Navy during Woodrow Wilson's administration, and gains critical experience in geopolitics while preparing the country for war at the outset of World War I.

1921
Roosevelt contracts polio, and battles furiously to regain the use of his legs. The fight consumes him for seven years, and he emerges from it with an increased compassion for the struggles of his fellow man.

1928
Roosevelt re-enters politics, runs for governor of New York State, and wins.

1932
Thirteen million people in the United States are out of work in the midst of the Great Depression when Franklin Delano Roosevelt is elected president. He sets off on a course of "bold, persistent experimentation."

1934
The Depression becomes so desperate and debilitating that a once-thriving and brilliant country begins to emit the sounds of revolution.

1936
"We are fighting," President Roosevelt says, "to save a great and precious form of government for ourselves and for the world." White House aide Harry Hopkins says of him, "There's something that he's got. It seems unreasonable at times, but he falls back on something that gives him complete assurance that everything is going to be all right."

1941
Roosevelt leads his country into World War II.

1944
As a catastrophic war subsides, Roosevelt turns to creating new ways for a world community to solve its differences: the United Nations. He dedicates significant resources to the rebuilding of countries ravaged by the war.

1945
Franklin Delano Roosevelt dies three weeks before the armistice at the end of World War II. His life has proved such a powerful beacon in world history that *The New York Times* chronicles his life in eight serialized parts.

GLIMPSES OF YOUTH

Franklin was homeschooled until he was fourteen years old.

"By the time I arrived at the meeting, the church was so filled up that a crowd of hundreds spilled out into the street, and speakers had to be set up outside to accommodate everyone. The excitement around the church was electrifying, and I remember having a sense that something powerful was being born. I squeezed my way through the crowd to my seat on a platform where a lively discussion about the boycott strategy was underway.... Then, Dr. King was introduced and began to speak in the rich, poised baritone and learned eloquence that distinguished even this debut speech of his career as a civil rights leader.... He said the words that I will never forget, the prophetic words that, for me, still define the character of our non-violent freedom movement. 'When the history books are written in the future, somebody will say, 'There lived a race of people, a black people, fleecy locks and black complexion, a people who had the moral courage to stand up for their rights. And thereby, they injected a new meaning into the veins of history and of civilization.'"

–ROSA LOUISE PARKS
A Call to Conscience: The Landmark Speeches of Dr. Martin Luther King, Jr.
by Clayborne Carson, Kris Shepard, and Andrew Young

"I look back on the days I spent with Mother Teresa in Calcutta as golden ones. Talking with her was a constant delight. She lets things out casually; that she bought a printing-press for the lepers so that they could print pamphlets and leaflets and make a little money. How, in God's name, I asked myself, did she know what press to buy and where to buy it? And with those stumps, how could the lepers hope to set type? Fatuous questions! The press is there and working; the lepers are delighted with it. She has, I found, a geography of her own–a geography of compassion. Somehow she hears that in Venezuela there are abandoned poor; so off the Sisters go there, and a house is set up. Then that in Rome–in this case, from the Pope himself–there are derelicts, as in Calcutta. Or again, that in Australia that aboriginals...need love and care. In each case, wherever it may be, the call is heard and answered."

–MALCOLM MUGGERIDGE
Something Beautiful for God

WITH VISION

"Men will thank God on their knees a hundred years from now that Franklin D. Roosevelt was in the White House. It was his hand, more than that of any other single man, that built the great coalition of the United Nations. It was his leadership which inspired free men in every part of the world to fight with greater hope and courage.

Gone is the fresh and spontaneous interest which this man took... in the troubles and the hardships and the disappointments and the hopes of little men and humble people."

–THE NEW YORK TIMES
editorial on Franklin Roosevelt's death

faith

1.
Confident belief in the
truth, value, or trust-
worthiness of a person,
idea, or thing

2.
Belief that does not rest
on logical proof or
material evidence

3.
A set of principles or
beliefs

com·pas·sion

1.
Deep awareness of the
suffering of another
coupled with the wish
to relieve it

vi·sion

1.
The faculty of sight

2.
Unusual competence
in discernment or
perception; intelligent
foresight

3.
The manner in which
one sees or conceives of
something

CHAPTER 3

A LEADER BECOMES A LEADER
FROM PASSION

"The most beautiful experience
that we can have is the mysterious.
It is the fundamental emotion that stands at the cradle
of true art and science. Whoever does not know it
and can no longer wonder, no longer marvel,
is as good as dead, and his eyes are dimmed."

−ALBERT EINSTEIN
visionary physicist

A LEADER BECOMES A LEADER
FROM PASSION

Johann Wolfgang von Goethe, the acclaimed German poet and writer of the eighteenth century, described the importance of tapping passion in driving a vision forward: "Whatever you can do or dream you can, begin it. Boldness has genius, power, and magic in it." Three centuries before, in a small village in Italy called Vinci, there lived a dark, bearded figure whose passions changed the way people lived and thought in the fifteenth century. He shimmered with an energy and talent that would fascinate people for centuries to come. A well-respected artist and writer of the time said of the mysterious figure, "Leonardo used to wear his hair and his beard so long and his eyebrows…so bushy that he appeared the very idea of noble wisdom."

Goethe and Leonardo da Vinci were figures possessed by the very genius, power, and magic that Goethe describes here. Both were filled with a boundless enthusiasm that we call passion. Each came to his village stage with staggering presence, changing the way people around them perceived the world through their timeless works: Goethe's drama *Faust* and da Vinci's *Mona Lisa*. "The heavens often rain down the richest gifts on human beings," a close friend of Michelangelo said, "but sometimes they bestow with lavish abundance upon a single individual beauty, grace, and ability, so that whatever he does, every action is so divine that he distances all other men, and clearly displays how his greatness is…not an acquirement of human art. Men saw this in Leonardo."

They saw it, too, in the lives of John Lennon, Billie Jean King, and César Chávez.

It is natural to wonder in what combination the heavens rain down these gifts, and in what proportion leaders reach up to their best dimensions. Those who stand out seem to capture a flood of energy that pours from their very core–from the insistent call to social justice that drove César Chávez, to the resolute need to accomplish that sets Billie Jean King apart in sports history.

Each leader's innate passion acts as an internal fire that ignites a young person to pursue goals that otherwise would seem impossibly out of reach. John Lennon sang late in his career, "Yes is the answer." It is an attitude that overwhelms the stuff of an ordinary life and drives an individual to the kind of passion and creative abundance that filled Lennon with a striking energy for art and living that made his short life an inspiration to so many.

Billie Jean King decided at just eleven years old that she would one day be the best tennis player in the world. "I just knew that day," she recalled years later, "after my first lesson that that was my destiny…. I got in the car…and said 'Hurry, hurry! I've got to tell Randall and Dad. I found out what I'm going to do with my life.'" It was a passionate beginning to an athletic and political life that would forever elevate the place of women in sports despite enormous physical odds and entrenched resistance.

In school, John Lennon turned the contempt he had for his father, who had deserted him when he was a young boy, into drawing, humor, and music. An internal rage drove him through adulthood after his father forced him to choose, when he was just five years old, between his mother and his father.

César Chávez was forever changed by the revulsion he felt for the men who cheated his father out of his family's business. After a desperate early life that included working as a teenager in sweltering fields to lift his family out of migrant poverty, he transmuted his pain into a passion and energy for political reform. Chávez ultimately changed the lives of the thousands of migrant farmers struggling in the fields of the American Southwest to survive. *The New York Times* explained the consequence of his lifetime of service: "Fighting growers and shippers who for generations had defeated efforts to unionize field workers, and later fighting rival unionists, Mr. Chávez for the first time brought a degree of stability and security to the lives of… migrant workers."

Such leaders transform personal struggles and pain into vibrant passions, and then transform those passions into shining results that cause us to wonder about the magnetic forces that created them. They choose to rise on the strength of "beauty, grace, and ability," rather than be pulled down by the struggle and suffering that might otherwise consume them. Their ability to rise despite the gravity of circumstance lights a path of redemption for themselves and for others—to admire, to understand, and to follow.

"If you want to remember me, organize," Chávez said. If you want to remember him, remind yourself that a simple resolute commitment from a passionate man can change a generation of people.

THE CREATIVITY OF
JOHN LENNON
1940-1980

"Yes is the answer."

–JOHN LENNON
artist and founder of the Beatles

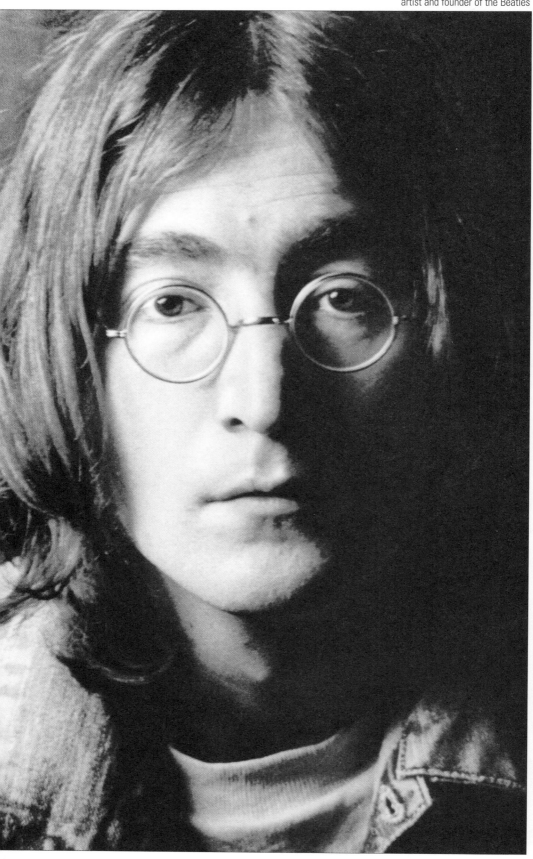

John Lennon became a leader in music,
writing songs that made people better people.

FROM PASSION

John Lennon was creativity in motion. It exuded from him, like a crystal waterfall–fluid, steady, constant, endless. In life, Lennon became a living icon for a way of being, for life as art. He brought to whatever he did a freshness, willingness, openness, inventiveness, frankness, grace, and magic. "Yes is the answer" was a famous lyric he wrote, an anthem his fans sang, and his simple but powerful way of life.

HE GRACED PEOPLE'S LIVES WITH THE POWER OF *YES*

He began creating, it seems, when he began. At an early age, he drew, sang, and invented ways of entertaining family and friends. In grammar school, he was always with pencil and paper, drawing, cartooning, writing prose and poetry, capturing vignettes of life around him. By age seventeen, he was into rock-and-roll (they called it Skiffle music), playing guitar, singing, writing, raving it up with friends from the neighborhood. At age thirty, already an ex-Beatle, he could turn simple things, like walking down the street, into something elegant, an opportunity to transform the moment. One famous home video clip has him two-stepping his way past the traffic with his wife Yoko, whisking her around in a glide of Liverpool charm and energy, like the English gentleman artist he had become–that fluid rush of hair pouring from him, almost leading the way.

And the Beatles, of course. The Beatles, the band that emerged from his first band, the Quarry Men, became one of the most remarkable forces in music history. John, Paul, George, and Ringo created thirteen masterpiece recordings in a short creative sprint of just nine years. In a 108-month creative explosion that set the music world reeling, they went from playing at the Cavern Club in Germany to the roof of the Apple Records Building in London for their live swan song. Few would ever experience music, television, film, live shows, walruses, submarines, or Norwegian wood the same way again.

Lennon fought his share of personal demons along the way. Turbulent bouts with drugs and alcohol, and a famous temper, all threatened to capsize him at various points. But his love for life, art, music, thought, Yoko, and just walking down the street, moved a generation to walk the streets with him – to "give peace a chance," to "imagine there's no countries," to "picture yourself in a boat on a river with tangerine dreams and marmalade skies." His charm, wit, style, and overflowing genius and talent put a generation around the world at ease during troubled times of war and change. He made you laugh, desire, smile, cry, care, despair, and question, all in time to a three-minute pop song.

His last waltz would be a walk back to the Dakota, the apartment building where he lived in New York City, from a recording session for his last album, *Double Fantasy*, in 1980. He was in the prime of life, just forty, returning to recording and public life after a long hiatus, and now a satisfied father of a five-year-old boy. Five shots from a crazed fan ended his life. The sidewalks of New York filled that night with the throngs who had walked with him during those magic years, and who had come to experience the transcendent power of their hero one more time. The power of his creativity and the legacy of his unrestrained imagination live on.

"And we all shine on, like the moon and the stars and the sun."

JOHN'S LIFE

1940
John Winston Lennon is born on October 9th, in Liverpool, England, to Alfred and Julia Lennon.

1943
John's father, Alfred, returns from his work as a merchant seaman to see his son for the first time. Soon, he will abandon the family after John's mother refuses to remake a life with him and to share custody.

1956
Lennon creates his first band, a Skiffle group called the Quarry Men.

1957
At age seventeen, John meets Paul McCartney, who comes to hear the Quarry Men play in concert. He recruits Paul to join the band.

1958
John Lennon's mother is killed by an off-duty police officer who is driving while intoxicated, leaving the young man without parents at age eighteen.

1960
The Quarry Men officially change their name to the Beatles.

1964
The Beatles tour the United States for the first time and make what will be an historic appearance on "The Ed Sullivan Show."

1967
The Beatles release *Sgt. Pepper's Lonely Hearts Club Band*, an album rock critics will hail as one of the most influential of all time.

1970
After a spectacular creative decade in which they create thirteen classic recordings, the Beatles dissolve their partnership. The Lennon-McCartney team has become one of the most dynamic songwriting forces in popular music history.

1971-1976
John and wife Yoko Ono become dynamic political activists, creating anti-war demonstrations and thought-provoking public displays that will galvanize the international community.

Lennon releases his classic solo album *Imagine*. John and Yoko retreat from public life for six years to raise their son, Sean.

1980
John and Yoko release *Double Fantasy*, an album that will outsell all of Lennon's post-Beatles solo efforts.

John is murdered on the Upper West Side of New York City on his apartment building steps.

GLIMPSES OF YOUTH

John Lennon spent a lot of class time in high school drawing grotesque caricatures of the school's teachers.

"Once social change begins, it cannot be reversed. You cannot uneducate the person who has learned to read. You cannot humiliate the person who feels pride. You cannot oppose the people who are not afraid anymore."

—CÉSAR CHÁVEZ
founder of the United Farm Workers

César Chávez became a leader in the fields fighting for people's right to make their lives better

FROM PASSION

They toiled in the fields under the most oppressive conditions–endless hours in the heat of an unrelenting California sun, breathing air ripe with cancer-causing pesticides, all of it for pay so low they were unable to afford the very food they were harvesting to market. Their employers provided no fresh water for them, no bathrooms, no care for their health problems, no breaks in the seven-day week–nothing, in short, to abate the hellish conditions. In some ways, it was a virtual slavery for the migrant workers of the American West, who roamed the countryside from job to job, struggling to keep ahead of an overwhelming, crushing, and relentless poverty.

HE HELPED THE POOREST AMONG US DRAW STRENGTH FROM THEIR NUMBERS

It would take passion, courage, and uncommon leadership to change the migrant workers' desperate condition. One of them who possessed these traits stood up, organized them, and in so doing, finally said, "Enough." His name was César Chávez.

In his time, no one believed that you could organize farm workers–they were just too poor, too powerless, too weary, too frightened, and too oppressed. But he led and lived by a single precept in Spanish–"Si se puede!" It means, "Yes, it can be done!"

In the beginning, Chávez organized two or three workers at a time, moving from farm to farm like a talented planter. From these initial memberships, he cultivated a collective that would become a powerful economic force–a labor union called the United Farm Workers. He banished hazardous pesticides from the fields on the strength of protest fasts, worker strikes, and national boycotts of grapes and lettuce. He improved the oppressive working conditions, slowly turning brutality and racism into respect and dignity in an alchemy of social justice, tilling the soil of social change in a way it had never been tilled before. His actions were both heroic and profound. He worked the ins and outs of power politics masterfully, combining skill and deep-rooted moral convictions into one common purpose. He improved the fortunes of thousands of oppressed people by dedicating his life to theirs–cultivating their dreams, and harvesting with them a different tomorrow.

César Chávez did his work with a farmer's rhythm, knowing that many seasons would have to come and go before the powerless would have safe and just working conditions. To demand a modicum of decency from the owners, he knew, would be a major step. But, "Si se puede!" The first boycott lasted five years before it achieved its intended result.

He said of the workers he represented so passionately: "It's ironic that those who till the soil, cultivate and harvest the fruit, vegetables, and other foods that fill your tables with abundance have nothing left for themselves." He said of the method the union implemented: "Nonviolence calls for hard-nosed organizing, for a minimum of dramatics, and a great deal of understanding of what the situation is." And he said of the profound and dramatic change and reform the union movement had begun: "Once social change begins, it cannot be reversed. You cannot uneducate the person who has learned to read. You cannot humiliate the person who feels pride. You cannot oppose the people who are not afraid anymore."

CÉSAR'S LIFE

1927
César Chávez is born on March 31st to Librado and Juana Chávez in Yuma, Arizona. He is their second child.

1937
The Chávez family loses its farm, as the Great Depression destroys family businesses around the United States. His father moves the Chávez clan west, where they will barely survive as migrant workers. César attends some thirty-eight different schools growing up.

1937-1946
The young Chávez leaves school in the eighth grade to work full-time as a laborer to help support his family. He experiences first-hand the oppressive conditions that exist for migrant workers and their families, and devotes himself, when he is not working, to a life of self-education. César's father teaches him early that to be successful is to work hard. His mother stresses the importance of compassion for the less fortunate.

1946
At age nineteen, Chávez joins the Navy and settles in the San Jose, California area. He leaves the military after two years and marries Helen Fabela. They will have eight children together.

1948-1953
During César Chávez's first years as an adult in San Jose, two mentors shape his future. A local priest introduces him to the teachings and philosophies of Mohandas Gandhi, a world leader who advocates methods for nonviolent social change. Fred Ross, a local advocate for social justice, teaches him important methods for organizing protests and galvanizing people to fight for equal rights and justice.

1953
Chávez joins Ross's Community Service Organization (the CSO), and rises to become its president. The organization is committed to eradicating discrimination based on race and class.

1962-1965
Chávez resigns from the CSO to found the National Farmworkers Association, an organization dedicated to economically disenfranchised farmworkers. His ability to adapt and creatively apply the nonviolent but highly effective methods of Gandhi bring him hard-won and, at times, stunning results.

1969
After seven years of intense organizing and protests, Delano, California growers sign an historic labor agreement with the United Farm Workers. For another two and a half decades, Chávez serves as the head of the UFW and advances critical work reforms in the form of fair wages, health insurance, and decent work conditions that radically change the quality of life for workers.

1993
Chávez dies in his sleep in San Luis, Arizona, near where he was born. In his life, he was presented his country's highest award, the Presidential Medal of Freedom. Yet he asked his followers to remember him simply–by organizing and protecting the rights of the least powerful.

GLIMPSES OF YOUTH

Because his family was itinerant, César Chávez, the founder of the United Farm Workers Union, went to thirty-eight different schools growing up.

THE RESILIENCE OF
BILLIE JEAN KING

1943-

"No matter how tough, no matter what kind of outside pressure, no matter how many bad breaks along the way, I must keep my sights on the final goal, to win, win, win–and with more love and passion than the world has ever witnessed in any performance."

–BILLIE JEAN KING
world champion tennis player

Billie Jean King became a leader in sport
challenging prejudice to make the world a better place

FROM PASSION

When Billie Jean King was just eleven, she had her first tennis lesson, returned home, and told her mother, "I want to play tennis forever. I'm going to be number one in the world."

That simple statement would be the start of an athletic legacy that would change the face of women's professional sports around the world. From the beginning, she played with a power, aggressiveness, and edge that had not been experienced in women's tennis, rushing the net with regularity and hitting the ball with unequalled power. As a professional, over the course of a storied career, she would win twenty Wimbledon championships, thirteen U.S. Open titles, and was ranked the number one women's player in the world five times.

SHE WON FOR WOMEN EVERYWHERE

But it was in working to change the stature of women that she would make her most significant mark.

That young girl's dream–being number one in the world in women's tennis–didn't mean much when she got her start. She was appalled to find that women athletes were dramatically underpaid and given unequal treatment in every regard.

When she began playing professionally in 1961, she noted that women's tennis was covered more on the society pages of newspapers than it was on the sports pages. It's hard to imagine a time when an athlete of Serena Williams's stature would not receive prominent media coverage, or compete for the same prize money as men, but that was the case for Billie Jean King, and for women athletes everywhere, when she first appeared at center court.

Billie Jean King knew instinctively that she had to fight fire with fire–that the only way to change people's minds was to do something dramatic. And so, when Bobby Riggs, a Wimbledon champion and vocal opponent of women's rights, badgered her into a singles match–best of five sets–to prove that no woman, not even the best in the world, could beat a man, it was an offer she couldn't refuse.

It started as a simple enough idea–the "Battle of the Sexes." But the event garnered international media attention beyond anyone's imagination, bringing to the Astrodome in Houston, Texas, where the match was played, a broadcast audience estimated at fifty million people.

Many women around the world sat breathless that night in front of their television sets as this lone warrior walked out onto center court, with the case for women's equality seeming to rest squarely on her shoulders, a simple racket serving as the means to an end that had vast economic and political repercussions.

Despite her fears that a loss would set the cause of women "back fifty years," she won handily, running Riggs ragged with the brilliance of her serves, groundstrokes, and charges to the net. The sheer pubic relations force of the event catapulted women's tennis onto the international stage. It would be years, and many more confrontations, before women would take home prizes somewhat equivalent to the men's, but the initial breakout moment in Houston opened up all the doors that had long been slammed shut.

The outspoken Olympian Willeye White said of her, "Today's young women athletes have no clue that they're where they are because of the courage of Billie Jean King." Frank Deford, a writer for *Sports Illustrated*, explained more fully: "She has prominently affected the way fifty percent of society thinks and feels about itself in a vast area of physical exercise. Moreover, like Arnold Palmer, she has made a whole sports boom because of the singular power of her personality."

"Within the apartment, John guided me through a hall covered with photographs to the kitchen, where he instructed me to wait while he freshened up. Yoko was off in a different part of the apartment. As I looked around the huge, freshly painted kitchen, stocked with containers of tea and coffee, spices and grains, I heard voices from a distant bedroom: a child's giggling and a father's mock scolding. 'So, you rascal, why are you asleep? Ahh haa! Well, I would have kissed you goodnight even if you were sleeping, silly boy.' John came tripping back into the kitchen, wholly revitalized, and while putting a pot of water on to boil, he explained that their child Sean wasn't used to his and Yoko's new schedule, working on the album all hours. Before this project, John had been home virtually all the time.... I smiled and continued: 'What have you been doing [since leaving the public eye in 1975]?'... 'I've been baking bread...and looking after the baby.'"

–DAVID SHEFF
All We Are Saying: The Last Major Interview with John Lennon and Yoko Ono

"My father used to say that the organizer's job is to help ordinary people do extraordinary things. He'd say that everyone in the movement has an important contribution to make, whether it's cooking in the strike kitchen or arguing in court–and it's the organizer's job to help them make that contribution.... He also had great faith in the decency of Americans, what he called 'our court of last resort.' He believed that if farm workers could offer a simple, nonviolent appeal for justice, the American people would respond.

By doing so, perhaps unwittingly, he also taught millions of Latinos and other Americans from all walks of life who never worked on a farm about the meaning of commitment and sacrifice for a cause larger than yourself."

–PAUL F. CHÁVEZ
president, National Farm Workers Service Center, Inc., September 18th, 2002, Washington, D.C.

FROM PASSION

"She was too good, she played too well.
She was playing well within herself,
and I couldn't get the most out of my game.
It was over too quickly.... She was never extended.
The girl was all over me the whole time."

–BOBBY RIGGS
tennis champion, on his famous loss to Billy Jean King
in the "Battle of the Sexes" in the Astrodome, Houston, 1973

cre·a·tiv·i·ty

1.
Characterized by
originality and
expressiveness;
imagination

de·cen·cy

1.
The quality or state of
being decent, suitable,
or becoming, in words
or behavior

2.
Proper formality

re·sil·ience

1.
The ability to recover
quickly from illness,
change, or misfortune;
buoyancy

2.
Irrepressible liveliness
and good spirit

CHAPTER 4

A LEADER BECOMES A LEADER
OF SERVICE

"When it is genuine,
when it is born of the need to speak,
no one can stop the human voice.
When denied a mouth, it speaks with the hands,
or the eyes, or the pores, or anything at all."

—EDUARDO GALEANO
from *Celebration of the Human Voice*

A LEADER BECOMES A LEADER
OF SERVICE

"If you want to be important, wonderful. If you want to be recognized, wonderful. But recognize that he who is greatest among you shall be your servant. That's a new definition of greatness."

He spoke to his audience that morning with his trademark fervor, which could make people believe a dream would last forever. But Dr. Martin Luther King, Jr. had grown world-weary by the morning of February 4th, 1968–frustrated and spent on a bloody road to achieving civil rights. Along the way, he had been stabbed; his family's home bombed; and his people savaged by police dogs, fire hoses, and crowds that were desperate to stop the insistent change that would not go away. Martin Luther King had come back to his father's church that morning, the Ebenezer Baptist Church in Atlanta, Georgia, to preach to a crowd hungry for meaning and answers. The man would be gone just two months later.

"Everyone can be great. Because everyone can serve. You don't have to have a college degree to serve. You don't have to make your subject and your verb agree to serve. You don't have to know about Plato and Aristotle to serve. You don't have to know Einstein's theory of relativity to serve. You don't have to know the second theory of thermodynamics in physics to serve. You only need a heart full of grace, a soul generated by love. And you can be that servant."

A towering man of service named Millard Fuller–the founder of Habitat for Humanity, who stands six feet, four inches tall–explained the concept of service with his own brand of clarity and resonance some twenty years later: "It's not your blue blood, your pedigree or your college degree. It's what you do with your life that counts."

Millard Fuller did with his life. When President Bill Clinton awarded him the Presidential Medal of Freedom in 1996 for his two decades of building Habitat for Humanity, he said, "I don't think it's an exaggeration to say that Millard Fuller has revolutionized the concept of philanthropy."

He started out at a young age, just twenty-nine, to change the art of giving. "The elimination of poverty housing in the world" would be his organization's goal, and the effort to house the homeless would eventually stretch from hand to hammer, and from hammer to nail, until thousands of followers in three thousand communities had built homes for more than a million people. Habitat volunteers would invent together a new measure of greatness, one nail and floor board at a time, on a balance sheet made from hope, selfless energy, and love. Fuller would face the problem of homelessness around the world with aplomb, persuasion, and resolve. "People of good will…should find it hard to rest in peace" in the face of widespread need, he said, and he inspired in thousands of others the same drive to overcome seemingly impossible odds. President Clinton said of his work: "Millard Fuller has done as much to make the dream of home-ownership a reality in our country and throughout the world as any living person."

Albert Schweitzer was thirty years old, and the dean of a college, when he was inspired to new directions and a life of service. He gave up a firmly established career as an acclaimed writer, concert organist, and academic before spending seven years becoming a medical doctor, and ultimately venturing overseas to Lambaréné, Africa, to start a hospital designed to support the health needs of a large local community.

Marian Wright Edelman, the founder of the Children's Defense Fund, started at age thirty-four to build an organization advocating the protection of children and the support of their developmental needs. From the beginning, her single goal was to help parents to raise their children in a world increasingly hostile to decency, safety, and prosperity for families. "If you don't like the way the world is," she said, emphasizing her mission, "you have an obligation to change it."

"Man's ethics must not end with man, but should extend to the universe," Schweitzer explained. "He must regain the consciousness for the great chain of life from which he cannot be separated. He must understand that all creation has its value…." His medical center in Lambaréné served two thousand sick people in the first nine months. "Everyone must find his own Lambaréné," Schweitzer said of his journey. Dr. King would add, "You only need a heart full of grace, a soul generated by love. And you can be that servant."

"The measure of our worth is inside our heads and our hearts."

–MARIAN WRIGHT EDELMAN
advocate for the rights of all children

Marian Wright Edelman became a leader in children's advocacy,
boldly finding solutions to children's problems, one solution at a time.

OF SERVICE

Her father was the Reverend Arthur Wright, a modest, unassuming, and powerful man who spent his life ministering to a segregated and struggling African-American community in Bennettsville, South Carolina, where she grew up. He was the kind of leader who built a park and roller skating rink behind his Baptist parish, because the people of his congregation were prohibited from enjoying the local public parks. In his eyes, it was the only right response to the injustice at hand. "That taught me," his daughter would later tell *Time* magazine, "if you don't like the way the world is, change it."

SHE MOVED CHILDREN TO THE TOP OF THE AGENDA

Marian Wright Edelman was so affected by the love, devotion, discipline, and self-sacrifice of her father that she made it her life's mission to bring the same level of care, concern, and protection to vulnerable and underprivileged children everywhere. The rationale behind her life's work has been pretty simple: "If we don't stand for children, then we don't stand for much." In 1973, at just thirty-four years old, she started a national crusade of "conscience and action" to "leave no child behind." She called it the Children's Defense Fund, and began to lobby tirelessly for the rights of every child—from access to the right educational resources and essential health care, to Head Start initiatives for pre-school kids and pregnancy prevention programs for teens.

It has been an organization that has had uncommon success. Senator Edward Kennedy has called Edelman "the 101st Senator on children's issues. She has real power in Congress and uses it brilliantly." The organization gained equal access to public education for handicapped children in the mid-1980s, and also succeeded in dramatically increasing Medicaid coverage for the most vulnerable and least protected. Edelman has faced harsh opposition along the way. Her critics have said she is too pedantic and preachy, and that her approach and philosophy rely too heavily on spending money to solve problems. Her response to naysayers: "We are punishing ourselves in escalating welfare, crime, and lost workers and productivity by failing to value, invest in, and protect all of our children."

Staggering challenges remain. In the United States alone, 13.5 million children live in poverty. Twelve million have no health care, and one hundred thousand are homeless. Fifty percent of the children in low-income families are not immunized from fatal yet preventable diseases. And four thousand die each year from handgun violence. Edelman understands the daunting nature of the mission at hand, and accepts it with uncommon compassion, and a shining ability to articulate her vision. Her powerful bestseller, *The Measure of Our Success: Letter to My Children and Yours*, opens a window on her world, pulling readers into the center of the children's advocacy work that she so adores. She has said of growing up, "It is not easy for anybody to grow up, to craft a purposeful role in the world, to develop a positive passion for life." On the commitment of parents, she says, "Parents for today's children must at all costs maintain a home, a center of love for their nurture and security…. The home—that should be the strongest link in education—is rapidly becoming the weakest." And she decries the times we live in: "Never have we exposed children so early and relentlessly to cultural messages glamorizing violence, sex, possessions, alcohol, and tobacco with so few mediating influences from responsible adults."

Memories of her father resonate in all that she has seen, like a cardinal in the backyard come to announce the arrival of another time. "I was fourteen years old the night my Daddy died," she recalls. "He had holes in his shoes, but two children out of college, one in college, another in divinity school, and a vision he was able to convey to me as he lay dying in an ambulance that I, a young black girl, could do anything; that race and gender are shadows; and that character, determination, attitude, and service are the substance of life."

Through her work, she has passed on her father's timeless vision to generations of children who do not have the opportunity to play and skate in parks like the one he built behind that church in Bennettsville, South Carolina.

MARIAN'S LIFE

1939
Marian Wright is born to Arthur Jerome and Maggie Leola Wright in Bennettsville, South Carolina.

1953
Her beloved father, Arthur, who has been her mentor and inspiration, dies when Marian is fourteen years old. His last words to her, in the back of an ambulance racing to the hospital, are, "Don't let anything get in the way of your education."

1953-1956
Marian attends racially segregated schools, and stands out in her studies. She enjoys music—singing and playing the piano—and becomes a drum majorette in the high school band.

1963
She graduates from Yale Law School and becomes the first African-American woman admitted to the Mississippi bar. She meets Peter Edelman, an assistant to Robert Kennedy, during a fact-finding tour of the slums of the Mississippi Delta, and falls in love with him. The couple marries, and has three sons.

1973
Marian Wright Edelman founds the Children's Defense Fund, an independently funded children's advocacy group, dedicated to protecting the civil rights and basic needs of the most vulnerable children and families.

1976-1987
Edelman is elected chairman of the board of Spelman College, her alma mater, and serves for eleven years.

1990
In a major legislative drive, the Children's Defense Fund successfully lobbies Congress to pass the Act for Better Child Care, which provides for more than three billion dollars in critical programs and support.

1993
Edelman publishes *The Measure of Our Success*, a best-selling guide to living, growing up, and raising kids in what she describes as an increasingly difficult and complex cultural environment.

2000
Edelman receives the Presidential Medal of Freedom, the highest civilian honor in the United States. U.S. President Bill Clinton says of her influence: "[Her voice] brought Robert Kennedy to Mississippi, helped to organize the Poor People's Campaign, inspired…thousands of other citizens, young and old, to join her through the years in [a] crusade that has… changed the future for millions of America's children."

2007
Edelman continues her advocacy work, raising awareness about "the needs of children and encourag[ing] preventive investment before they get sick, into trouble, drop out of school, or suffer family breakdown."

GLIMPSES OF YOUTH

As Marian Wright Edelman and her four siblings grew up and began to leave home, her parents began adopting foster children. They would bring in twelve foster kids in all.

"I would consider myself justified
in living until I was thirty for science and art in order to devote myself
from that time forward to the direct service of humanity."

—ALBERT SCHWEITZER
scholar, doctor, and humanitarian

Albert Schweitzer became a leader,
dedicating his life to a concern for all living creatures.

OF SERVICE

Albert Schweitzer was so talented in such a variety of disciplines that his most difficult challenge was deciding where to focus his energies. By the time he was just thirty, he had become a world-class concert organist, a successful author, and a distinguished interpreter of the works of Johann Sebastian Bach. He was a recognized philosopher, thinker, and historian. He had been appointed the dean of a college. And in his spare time, he had become such a proficient restorer of antique pipe organs that his reputation for breathing life back into the most distressed of instruments preceded him. Working to revive an organ was, he believed, simply "part of the struggle for truth."

HE MEASURED SUCCESS IN BUNDLES OF TRUTH

He approached the things he did with a craftsman's attention to detail, and the passion of a consummate artist. "The biggest impression of Albert Schweitzer was of a man who had learned to use himself fully," Norman Cousins would write of him. "Physically, socially, spiritually, Schweitzer had never been a stranger to his potential." He was motivated by a reverence for life–a philosophy that he would eventually make the core of his guiding ethos. The essence of the teaching was that all living creatures deserved the greatest respect and reverence. He would become one of the first advocates for the rights of animals.

And then, as gracefully as he had risen to touch pieces of the sky in those early years, he left it all behind at the age of thirty to pursue a vision of human healing in Africa, a place where he had never been, and in a field of medicine that was completely new to him. The meaning he was searching for was now to be found across an ocean, on a different continent. His memoirs shed light on what was an extraordinary and unexpected change in his course: "As far back as I can remember, I was saddened by the amount of misery around me. I could not help thinking continuously of others denied… happiness by their material circumstances or their health…. I would consider myself justified in living until I was thirty for science and art in order to devote myself from that time forward to the direct service of humanity." To many observers, it was as if the all-embracing sense of responsibility that drove him had suddenly perverted his vision, and taken him away from a fantastic life of high achievement. People feared that this beautiful mind had suddenly collapsed of its own intense weight, to destroy the man they had come to know.

He set out, nonetheless, to spend seven years becoming a physician. He built a team, and then a hospital, in the remote village of Lambaréné, Africa, thousands of miles from his home. Lack of funds, difficulty in recruiting experienced people, and extraordinary physical fatigue filled the days with constant struggle. New plateaus only served to underscore how difficult the challenge had been: "For the first time since I came to Africa, my patients are housed as human beings should be. How I have suffered all these years from having to pen them together in stifling, dark rooms!"

Triumph would appear in the midst of the mammoth struggle. The spirit of the villagers, and of the Westerners who came to Lambaréné, combined to build a facility that was unique to the indigenous culture, and that outlasted every major obstacle. People who had suffered for years with disabling maladies came to the new healing center. And the truths of Albert Schweitzer emerged with new power, as the man who had renounced it all to live a life of freedom in service seemed to merge with the young Schweitzer who had soared on the wings of culture. An observer watched as the now-old doctor sat at the hospital's broken-down organ, and began to play his beloved instrument once again: "The impression of tremendous energy that he creates accords with his outward appearance: a tall, broad-shouldered robust figure to which it is easy to ascribe intellectual as well as physical heroism; it is an unforgettable sight to see this tall, powerful man approach the organ, put on his glasses and bend lovingly over the keys of the instrument in devoted service to his great master Bach. To see him is to see him suddenly transformed into the simple, earnest organist of bygone years."

1875
Albert Schweitzer is born in Kayserberg, Germany. His father is a minister; his grandfather, a classical organist.

1880-1890
As a young boy, Schweitzer displays a passion for playing the organ. In 1884, at nine years old, he first plays the organ in his father's church.

1893-1900
Schweitzer spends seven years in formal university training at the Sorbonne and the University of Berlin. He receives advanced degrees in theology and philosophy, and, on the side, becomes a master builder of organs.

1902
At twenty-seven, Dr. Schweitzer is appointed dean of St. Thomas College in Strasbourg.

1905
Schweitzer authors a seminal biography of Johan Sebastian Bach. That same year, he shocks family and friends with news that he will leave his career in music and academia to become a doctor. His goal is to open a free hospital in Lambaréné, Africa.

1913
After spending much of his thirties in medical school, Schweitzer launches an innovative hospital in Lambaréné with minimal funding. A chicken coop serves as part of the initial compound.

1917
Dr. and Mrs. Schweitzer are interned as prisoners of war during World War I. They are released in 1918.

1918-1924
Dr. Schweitzer writes five books and travels in Europe, lecturing, playing organ concerts, and taking additional medical courses.

1920
In a lecture in Sweden, Schweitzer describes a revelatory moment: "There flashed upon my mind the phrase 'reverence for life.' Man's ethics must not end with man, but should extend to the universe. He must regain the consciousness of the great chain of life from which he cannot be separated."

1924-1965
Dr. Schweitzer and his wife, Helen, return to Lambaréné to spend the next four decades building the hospital.

1965
Albert Schweitzer dies at the age of ninety. His legacy of selfless service was succinctly captured in the commendation given when he was awarded the Nobel Peace Prize in 1953:
"He has shown us that a man's life and his dream can be one. His work has made the concept of brotherhood a living one, and his words have reached and taken root in the minds of countless men."

THE GUMPTION OF
MILLARD FULLER

1935-

"All…people should have at least a simple, decent place to live."

—MILLARD FULLER
founder of Habitat for Humanity

Millard Fuller became a leader,
inventing new avenues for generosity and service.

OF SERVICE

"All…people should have at least a simple, decent place to live." He said it so easily, as if he were talking about building a science center for the local community's high school.

But Millard Fuller was talking about solving the complex problem of homelessness and poverty housing. The United Nations Centre for Human Settlements estimates that more than a billion people worldwide–about twenty percent of the world's population–wake up every day without a safe and healthy place to live. In 1976, Millard Fuller and his wife decided that they could not wake up every day without doing something about the problem. And so they began.

HE USED GUMPTION TO HOUSE THE WORLD

They began with a name: Habitat for Humanity. They began with an exuberant and far-reaching idea: that people volunteering under the umbrella of an innovative home building program could partner with individuals who needed housing, and deliver a solution around the world–in diverse countries, cultures, and communities.

Fuller's actions and bold experiment in innovative volunteerism and home building has, for three decades, set in motion volunteers in more than eighty countries who are making the problem go away. They are working to build houses for homeless people with the ultimate objective of putting a roof over the head of every person and family.

Visionary leaders, it is said, are able to make their vision of the future inevitable. The future of Habitat for Humanity began in Zaire in 1973 from a simple conversation between a man and a woman. Millard Fuller and his wife, Linda, were struggling in the midst of a trial separation in their young marriage. They had lost their way, even as they had become wealthy and successful in a burgeoning business. They found insufficient meaning and balance in the midst of the very goals and objectives they had set for themselves at the beginning.

And so they developed a new vision of success and fulfillment for themselves personally, and also for their married life. They regrouped, rejoined in New York City, and decided together to look at the landscape from a new perspective. "What would make life meaningful?" they asked themselves. Easing humanity's suffering by housing the people, they decided.

They gave up their wealth. They gathered volunteers. And they began. The concept was simple: to build homes using volunteer labor, donated materials, and interest-free loans.

Today, Habitat for Humanity operates in over eighty countries around the world. The organization has built two hundred thousand homes for families, many of whom are astonished by a house that seems to come from nowhere. Teams of volunteers fly in from around the world, on their own time, and build, in partnership with the host family, shelter from the storm. All told, more than a million people have received homes this way.

Call it daring. Call it gumption. Millard Fuller not only has it, he has been able to inspire it in the people around him with a story of hope that has literally changed the landscape of home ownership.

How does it happen? The founder answers this way: "The simplest answer I can offer to the question of how to eliminate poverty housing in the world is to make it a matter of conscience. We must do whatever is necessary to cause people to think and act to bring adequate shelter to everyone. And we do this through a spirit of partnership."

MILLARD'S LIFE

1935
Millard Fuller is born in a small cotton mill town in Lanett, Alabama. His mother dies when he is just three years old.

1960
Fuller graduates from the University of Alabama Law School, and starts a business with a classmate. His goal is to become wealthy at a young age. Although he makes the business very successful by the time he is just twenty-nine years old, the obsessive hours he puts in to achieve his goal consume him.

1965
Fuller finds his business thriving, but his marriage failing. His wife, Linda, leaves him, and the couple spends time rethinking the basic precepts of how they live their lives.

1973
Fuller and his wife recreate many of their marriage's underpinnings, and decide to leave the business that Millard built to dedicate their lives to creating Habitat for Humanity.

The goal is far-reaching: "to eliminate poverty housing in the world." To reach it, they create an innovative economic model in which families that don't have sufficient housing partner with the organization to build themselves homes.

1976
The Fullers found Habitat for Humanity International and open its headquarters in Americus, Georgia.

1989
Some fifteen years into the project, Habitat for Humanity increases its output of homes from two thousand a year to four thousand a year. *Time* magazine profiles the organization, and asks Fuller how Habitat can possibly wipe out the problem of homelessness. Fuller answers with his Southern candor and humility: "Man, we're just whittling away."

1996
U.S. President Bill Clinton awards Millard Fuller the Presidential Medal of Freedom. Presenting the award, the President says, "I don't think it's an exaggeration to say that Millard Fuller has literally revolutionized the concept of philanthropy."

2007
The organization has succeeded in housing more than 750,000 people in some three thousand communities. Fuller's simple philosophy–"I see life as both a gift and a responsibility"– galvanizes a mission that remains audacious in its goal of providing decent affordable housing for all people.

GLIMPSES OF YOUTH

Growing up in Alabama, Millard Fuller had a strong aversion to the tenements that many African-American sharecroppers made their homes.

His mission later in life with Habitat for Humanity was to rid the world of the kinds of shacks he saw early on, and to provide decent housing for every human being.

"I was fourteen years old the night my Daddy died.
He had holes in his shoes but two children out of college,
one in college, another in divinity school, and a vision
he was able to convey to me as he lay dying in an ambulance
that I, a young black girl, could be and do anything;
that race and gender are shadows; and that character,
self-discipline, determination, attitude, and service
are the substance of life."

—MARIAN WRIGHT EDELMAN
The Measure of Our Success: Letter to My Children and Yours

"He goes his way calmly, is full of humor,
has an extraordinary sense of adaptation, but also a mysterious shyness.
In everything he undertakes, he is animated by an incredible gentleness,
and an all-embracing sense of responsibility.... Respect for life!
Respect for all that breathes. In this idea, Schweitzer sees the real solution
of the question of the relationship of man to the world."

—GEORGE SEAVER
Albert Schweitzer: The Man and His Mind

OF SERVICE

"Habitat for Humanity is
the most successful continuous community service project
in the history of the United States. It has revolutionized the lives of
thousands.... Millard Fuller has done as much to make the dream of
home ownership a reality in our country and throughout
the world as any living person."

—WILLIAM JEFFERSON CLINTON
42nd president of the United States,
awarding Millard Fuller the Presidential Medal of Freedom

char·ac·ter

1.
The combination of
qualities or features
that distinguishes one
person, group, or thing
from another

2.
Moral or
ethical strength

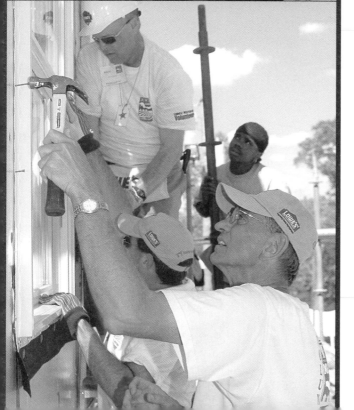

truth

1.
A statement proven to
be or accepted as true

2.
Sincerity, integrity

3.
That which is
considered to be the
supreme reality and to
have the ultimate
meaning and value
of existence

gump·tion

1.
Boldness of enterprise;
initiative or
aggressiveness

2.
Guts, spunk, moxie

3.
Common sense

CHAPTER 5

A LEADER BECOMES A LEADER
IN TRUTH

"Truth has no special time of its own.
Its hour is now."

—ALBERT SCHWEITZER,
scholar, doctor, and humanitarian

A LEADER BECOMES A LEADER
IN TRUTH

Mohandas Gandhi called his autobiography *Experiments with Truth,* having spent a lifetime developing in himself an ever-expanding capacity for integrating what he came to understand truth to be. "Truth is the substance of morality," he wrote. "Truth was becoming my sole objective. It began to grow in magnitude every day, and my definition of it has…been ever widening."

One of his disciples and closest confidants, Mahadev Desai, observed in him a fundamental trait: "Most of us think in one way and speak in another way and act in yet another way. Not so with [Gandhi].… He said what he believed and put in practice what he said, so his mind, spirit, and body were in harmony."

This legendary liberator of hundreds of millions, who led two vast peoples in South Africa and India to freedom, began with an essential principle: that leadership is a result of character, and that the fundamental building block of character is an abiding adherence to truth.

Leaders who seek to embody truth–in its core and varied dimensions–can develop in themselves a marked capacity to connect to the vivid struggles of our collective human drama.

Bob Marley developed a fervent belief that truth in spirit could set an impoverished people free–first in song, then in mind, then in body. As a prophet singing from the depths of despair in Trenchtown, Jamaica, one of the world's most desperate places, he lifted himself to a high place where he could see the sanctity and deliverance that he promised to all those within the sound of his voice: "Open your eyes and look within. Are you satisfied with the life you're living?" he sang. "We know where we're going. We know where we're from. We're leaving Babylon. We're going to the fatherland."

He fought his battles from a crossroads where culture and politics met, and brought to the world a vision of how people can overcome the most desperate conditions.

Where Bob Marley was inspired by the poverty and injustice he experienced growing up, Winston Churchill rose to truth when an uncommon international crisis erupted to engulf the European community.

In the 1930s, when an evil political philosophy began to set Europe on fire, Churchill saw in the movement's earliest footsteps the decided markings of tyranny's jackboot. From 1933 to 1945, it would seek to destroy all people who had attained any semblance of freedom. As prime minister of the United Kingdom, he called his country and its allies to arms early in the conflagration, and his prescience earned him revulsion from many political corners. People thought him alarmist at the beginning, but then proffered praise as his ability to see the truth in what was happening became apparent. Churchill proved an early voice in the wilderness to whom free people would rally.

As a biologist seeking to understand the effects of poisonous chemicals on people's health, Rachel Carson saw adherence to truth as a matter of human survival. She was an American ecologist and writer working in the 1930s, '40s, and '50s who presented a critical new vision of environmental science in a way that a broad audience could understand.

She taught the world about new scientific concepts in clear language that had a wide-reaching and shattering effect: the human body, she explained, was permeable, and could be poisoned by chemicals in its environment, a notion that was altogether surprising, and that would be rejected by the consensus of her time. Up until then, industry had unleashed chemicals into the environment indiscriminately, and disposed of its poisonous waste in unregulated fashion, as if the planet had an endless capacity to renew itself. People, plants, and animals all suffered the effects of a torrent of chemical and industrial pollution. And then, Carson released her seminal work, *Silent Spring*.

The release of this landmark book in 1962 has created a wellspring of desire in people around the world to better understand humankind's relationship to its environment. It is an ongoing search that has fascinated activists, citizens, and scholars alike. The issues Carson raised in her books ring true many decades after she first brought them to the fore so eloquently.

"It was the nation…that had the lion's heart.
I had the luck…to give the roar."

—WINSTON CHURCHILL
former Prime Minister of the United Kingdom

Winston Churchill became a leader in the 1940s,
standing up and saying things that were right, but hard to say.

IN TRUTH

As a teenager, he had a vision that he shared with close friends: he would lead the free world in its greatest hour of need, and save it from a towering tyrannical force. Even more unusual than having such a vivid vision at such a young age is that Winston Churchill grew up to fulfill it as prime minister of the United Kingdom during World War II.

HE BROUGHT ENGLAND TO ITS FINEST HOUR

You would not have predicted such a life from his beginnings. He was so rebellious a child that his teachers uniformly gave him negative marks, and some believed that he was incorrigible. He was at times so inward, and at other times so aggressive, that his mood swings and attitude changes frightened his parents and his classmates. He was a boy who revered his father, an English nobleman. And although his father admired his strange and gifted son, he was also sufficiently alienated by the distressing inner turmoil the young boy exhibited that he feared for his future. And so, Winston Churchill grew up at the turn of the nineteenth century, one part genius exploring his world and one part social exile, distanced from and misunderstood by those who were closest to him.

The internal conflict raged during adolescence, but he learned to channel the powerful energies into productive endeavors–he became a voracious reader, a thinker, an athlete, and a friend to fellow students. His passion for life and his varied abilities seemed to erupt like a geyser from a deep well of physical and emotional pain. He battled depression for much of his life. He struggled with bronchial infections, and the resulting fevers nearly killed him. But it was in these very battles to survive, as a boy and a teenager, that he would find himself. The resulting personal triumphs would create in him a spirit that would eventually lift the world's people during the darkest period of their history. His political statements–sometimes he was a startling voice in the wilderness–would serve throughout his adult life to crisply capture moments in history: "Never give in–never, never, never, never…never give in."

Over the course of his adult life, Churchill became an accomplished humorist, military man, leader, artist, pilot, farmer, polo player, and horse-breaker. He became one of the most dynamic leaders of his time, replacing Neville Chamberlain as prime minister of Great Britain in 1940–just in time to save the free world from the tyranny of the Nazis.

To remember his greatness is to remember the political obstacles that stood in the way of rallying the free world against the Nazis in what would be the most important war in recorded history. As nations were conquered, and peoples were brutally subjugated and murdered *en masse* because of their religious or ethnic identities, many countries failed to act. Churchill wrote of them: "They go on in strange paradox, decided only to be undecided, resolved only to be irresolute…all powerful to be impotent." It was only in acting, in fighting this monumental war, that the world would find a resolution to the deep horror that had been unleashed. "This is only the beginning of the reckoning," he wrote. "This is only the first sip, the first foretaste of a bitter cup…unless by a supreme recovery of moral health and martial vigor, we rise again and take our stand for freedom."

The child who struggled to connect with his own family became a man whose instincts, intellect, and power of expression united the Allied countries in the common purpose of defeating one of civilization's most destructive adversaries. We look back and honor his foresight, his leadership, and his resolve. We recall his powers as a speaker, leader, and politician. We recall in equal measure his dedication to the power of language and his vivid sense of humor. U.S. President John F. Kennedy saluted Churchill with the words: "He mobilized the English language and sent it into battle." Kennedy's words serve to remind us that one of Churchill's great victories was to harness the power of our essential humanity in a time of grave crisis–but only after Churchill, himself, had first spent years developing his own inner strength. "Character may be manifested in the great moments," he explained, "but it is made in the small ones."

1945-1981

"What life has taught me I would like to share
with those who want to learn…that until the basic human rights
are equally guaranteed to all…everywhere is war."

—BOB MARLEY
reggae artist and symbol of freedom

Bob Marley became a leader in Jamaica
by giving voice to an entire people.

IN TRUTH

The *New York Times* called him "the most influential artist of the second half of the 20th century." Robert Farris Thompson, an acclaimed art history professor at Yale University, said of him, "He was, quite simply, a William Shakespeare for modern times."

HE GAVE VOICE TO A PEOPLE

Bob Marley was an artist, philosopher, athlete, freedom-fighter, poet, musician, songwriter, and visionary. He was a singer who gave voice to millions of Africans and Jamaicans by singing their truths and speaking their minds in one famously resonant voice that delivered "melodies pure and true." He was a mystic, Jamaica's rebel music man, rasta man, reggae man, worldly man, creating man, father to eleven kids, and also to a set of ideas that have carried Jamaican and African adherents to higher ground, better understanding, and deeper connection. His songs made the world's radio get up, stand up, rise up and dance, while his words captured piercing human truths that made people's hair stand up like his dreadlocks, as the world listened to his clarion calls for greater justice, far-reaching peace, and fundamental transformation.

Marley grew up in one of the world's most desperate slums, Jamaica's Trenchtown. A loner, moody, and most comfortable in the gentle companionship of his guitar, he rose from his beginnings on homemade instruments made of bamboo shoots, electric cable, and oversized sardine cans. He rose on personal strength, navigating through the town's teenage toughs using native instinct and well-honed street smarts to defend himself. And he rose on the faith of the Jamaican people who had so very little, but invested in him so much–their hopes, their faith, and their vision for a shining place on the other side of despair and poverty.

His truths in music were reggae powerful and Rasta simple. Bob Marley charmed with a graceful, innocent, childlike clarity: "Oh, please. Don't you rock my boat. 'Cause I don't want my boat to be rockin'." His vision pierced the walls of racial separation and brought the people together through the strength of one voice and one joyous sound. For Jamaica, he was a political, spiritual, and musical force all in one man, whose attentions were sought by the most powerful politicians and who, as an international symbol of freedom and peace, threatened the very walls of Babylon. Once he became powerful, assassins came after him with their bullets. But nothing, not even the cancer that took his life at thirty-six, could end the flourishing and wide-ranging reach of his expansive vision for all humankind.

Just four days after the assassination attempt in 1976, Marley surprised everyone by keeping a scheduled appearance at the Smile Jamaica concert in a park in Kingston. Unable to pick up his guitar because of his recent wounds, he sang "War!" for the eighty thousand assembled: "What life has taught me I would like to share with those who want to learn… that until the basic human rights are equally guaranteed to all…everywhere is war."

Days before he would die of cancer, he would appear on national television to sing his anthem, "Redemption Song": "How long shall they kill our prophets while we stand aside and look. They say we're just a part of it. We've gotta fulfill the book."

And on his acclaimed single "Exodus," his voice rang out triumphant with the line, "Send us another Brother Moses. Gonna cross the Red Sea."

For his people, he was that brother, unassuming in his dreads, denim, and guitar, pulling the people across the sands of political, physical, and spiritual change. He brought to them the word of Rasta in song and carried its principles of moral uprightness, tolerance, and brotherhood over the seas for all the world to hear.

1945
Bob Marley is born
Robert Nesta Marley to Norval Marley and Cedellar Booker at Nine Miles, St. Ann's, Jamaica. His parents are of two different races, which will mark him as an outsider to Jamaican society.

1962
Bob leaves school at just fourteen years old to pursue his love of music, and an interim trade in welding.

1963
Marley forms the Wailers with several Trenchtown friends.

1964
The Wailers release their first single, "Simmer Down," which powers to number one on the Jamaican pop charts.

1966
Bob marries Rita, who will be his wife until his early death in 1981. The couple opens a record store in Kingston, Jamaica.

1968
Marley's interest in Rastafarianism as a philosophy and a way of life begins.

1970
The Wailing Wailers release their classic album, *Soul Rebel*.

1972
The Wailers sign with Island Records, and soon thereafter release *Catch a Fire* in 1973.

1974
Eric Clapton records Marley's classic, "I Shot the Sheriff." The single rockets to number one in the United States. Marley's musical renown spreads far outside Jamaica.

1976
Gunmen believed to be politically motivated break into Marley's Kingston home, shooting him, members of his family, and his associates. He plays the Smile Jamaica Festival four days later.

1977
Bob Marley is first diagnosed with cancer.

1978
Bob Marley and the Wailers play the One Love Peace concert in Kingston, and Marley works to create peace by bringing together the country's rival political bosses in an embrace on stage.

1981
Bob Marley dies at thirty-six at Cedars of Lebanon Hospital in Miami. A national holiday is created on his birthday in Jamaica in 1990.

1984
Island Records releases *Legend*, a chronicle of the music of Bob Marley and the Wailers that will top international charts and become the best-selling reggae album in history.

Bob Marley grew up in Trenchtown, one of the world's poorest ghettos. He would go on to make the place famous in songs like "Trenchtown" and "No Woman No Cry." He released a first song, "Simmer Down," with his group, the Wailing Wailers, at 17 years old.

"Those who contemplate the beauty of the earth
find resources of strength that will endure as long as life lasts."

–RACHEL CARSON
zoologist, author, and environmental visionary, quoting Jean Rostand

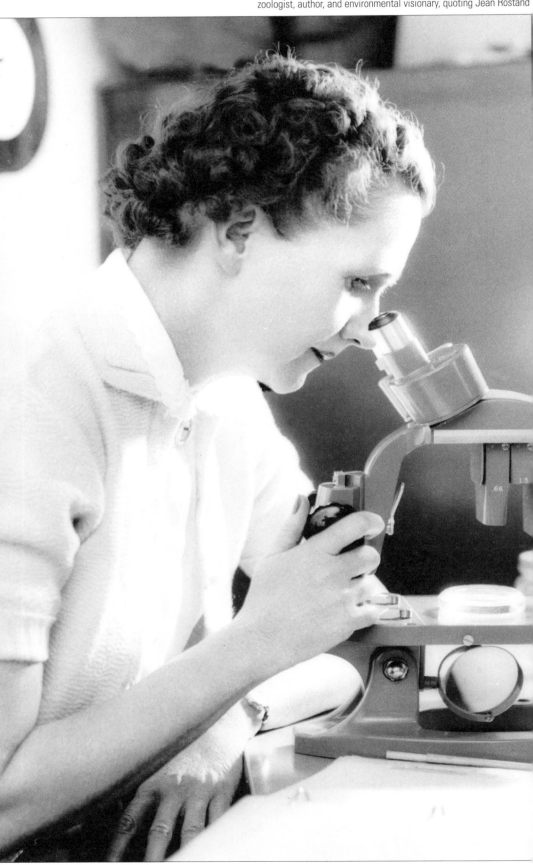

Rachel Carson became a leader b
championing the most powerful ideas in simple terms

IN TRUTH

"If a child is to keep alive his inborn sense of wonder," Rachel Carson wrote, "he needs the companionship of at least one adult who can share it, rediscovering with him the joy, excitement, and mystery of the world we live in." She wrote those words, in an essay called "The Sense of Wonder," to emphasize the importance of exposing children to the majesty of the natural world. She wrote it so that others would experience what she did as a little girl growing up on a farm in Allegheny County, Pennsylvania: a landscape of rural mystery and joy, where she had filled her childhood days with the colors of the outdoors that seemed to crackle all around against the "beauty overhead."

SHE STARTED A MOVEMENT TO SAVE THE LIVING WORLD

She was a woman who was in love with nature, as well as a marine biologist and writer whose voice and visionary insights about preserving the natural world and the natural order were so profound that they would one day be heard around the world. Her seminal work, *Silent Spring*, released in 1962, revolutionized the way people conceive of humanity's place in nature by demanding that the makers of progress be held accountable. She wanted people to understand the risk toxic waste presented to their health. "We are subjecting whole populations to exposure to chemicals which animal experiments have proved to be extremely poisonous and in many cases cumulative in their effect," she explained.

At the time she wrote it in the early 1960s, no one questioned the right of industrial companies to expand at any pace. Industrial society had brought with it a level of prosperity that seemed to have no limit, and it was not for the faint of heart to critique the fundamentals of a prospering economy. After a mosquito-control campaign in 1957 near Duxbury, Massachusetts, devastated area birds and wildlife, she felt that time was of the essence, and that she had enough ammunition to act. The opposition that she encountered to *Silent Spring* was vast. Her adversaries in the industrial-chemical complex had extraordinary resources, and did their best to marginalize her position. Dr. Robert White-Stevens, a spokesman for the chemical industry, held the majority view: "The crux, the fulcrum over which the argument chiefly rests, is that Miss Carson maintains that the balance of nature is a major force in the survival of man, whereas the modern chemist, the modern biologist and scientist, believes that man is steadily controlling nature."

Rachel Carson was not a radical; she understood that a responsible use of chemicals would be an integral part of modern society. But as a visionary, writing at first in relative obscurity, this solitary woman would change the consciousness of millions of people, and start the environmental movement. She explained truths as jolting as Newton's: first, that human bodies are not separate but permeable, and affected by environmental pollutants; and second, that although the human race is important, it is only a part in a vast ecosystem that needs protection and balance to prosper and grow.

Her ideals set the world on a track to pursue the course of environmental responsibility. She is a case study of an individual whose personal convictions and values changed the very course of society. "Man is a part of Nature," she told CBS television, "and his war against Nature is inevitably a war against himself."

We remember Rachel Carson most clearly as a woman who understood the power of what was at stake, and who could powerfully translate that understanding to a world audience in no uncertain terms: "The stormy Autumn night when my nephew Roger was about twenty months old, I wrapped him in a blanket and carried him down to the beach in the rainy darkness," she wrote. "Out there, at the edge of where we couldn't see, big waves were thundering in, dimly seen white shapes that boomed and shouted and threw great handfuls of froth at us. Together, we laughed for pure joy–he a baby meeting for the first time the wild tumult Oceanus, I with the salt of half a lifetime of sea love in me. But I think we felt the same spine-tingling response to the vast, roaring ocean and the wild night around us."

1907
Rachel Carson is born to Robert Warden Carson and Maria McLean Carson in Springdale, Pennsylvania.

1908-1914
She grows up the youngest of three children on an expanse of sixty-five acres in rural Springdale, where her mother imbues her with an emphatic joy in, and appreciation for, the outdoors. She shows an unusual capacity for expressing herself. The subject of her early writings is often her fascination with nature.

1914-1927
Rachel's home life is strained, as her father struggles to make ends meet, and her parents battle about their difficulties. She learns to earn money early to help the family survive. Her outdoor world becomes a sanctuary from the pressures of family life.

1932
Carson does research at the Woods Hole Marine Biological Institute, and then receives her master's degree in zoology from Johns Hopkins University.

1941
The thirty-four-year old Carson becomes editor-in-chief of all of the publications for the U.S. Fish and Wildlife Services.

1951
Carson publishes *The Sea Around Us*, an international bestseller that opens for a mass audience a window on the mysteries and majesty of the ocean, as well as the ocean's importance to the earth's ecosystem.

1962
The Sea Around Us will ultimately be translated into thirty languages. Carson publishes *Silent Spring*. It is rare that a book changes history, but *Silent Spring* does just that.

Its basic thesis that human bodies are permeable and can be poisoned by pesticides and other man-made poisons is so radical and threatening to people's sense of security that many point to the book's publication as the *de facto* beginning of the modern environmental movement.

1963
President Kennedy's Science Advisory Committee publishes a thoroughly researched pesticide report that affirms many of the core tenets of Carson's writings. It proves compelling evidence to counter the vicious attacks that the chemical industry has leveled at the acclaimed author. *Silent Spring* becomes another bestseller for Carson.

The Columbia Broadcasting System debuts a show that profiles Carson's work. In it, Carson explains the drama the human species faces: "We still haven't become mature enough to think of ourselves as only a tiny part of a vast and incredible universe."

1964
Rachel Carson dies after a long battle with cancer.

As a teenager, Carson believed, she could not both write and pursue marine biology at the same time. Her later triumphs would prove this early assumption wrong.

"Churchill had become an aggressive extrovert, but at the same time he had developed into a rare type–C.G. Jung called it the 'extroverted intuitive'–and it was that, not his surface toughness, that changed the history of the world. Jung wrote: '[The extroverted intuitive] has a keen nose for things in the bud, pregnant with future promise.' That…is what C.P. Snow had in mind when he wrote: 'Judgment is a fine thing: but it is not all that uncommon. Deep insight is much rarer. Churchill had flashes of that kind of insight…. When Hitler came to power, Churchill did not use judgment but one of his deep insights. That was what we needed…. Plenty of people on the left could see the danger; but they did not know how the country needed to be seized and unified.' The answer was found by an extroverted intuitive. In Jung's description of the type, 'his capacity to inspire his fellow-men with courage, or to kindle enthusiasm for something new, is unrivaled.' Field Marshal Alanbrooke, Churchill's chief of the Imperial General Staff, was constantly astonished by his 'method of suddenly arriving at some decision as it were by intuition, without any kind of logical examination of the problem…. He preferred to work by intuition and by impulse.' Jan Christiaan Smuts said: 'That is why Winston is indispensable.'"

–WILLIAM MANCHESTER
The Last Lion: Winston Spencer Churchill: Visions of Glory, 1874-1932

"Marley murmured that he would sing one song…['War!']…
At the close of his performance, Bob began a ritualistic dance, acting out aspects of the ambush that had almost taken his life…. Swaying slowly and half-steppin' to the beat, Bob opened his shirt and rolled up his left sleeve to show his wounds to the world.

The last thing they saw before the reigning King of Reggae disappeared back into the hills was the image of the man mimicking the two-pistoled fast draw of a frontier gun slinger, his locks thrown back in triumphant laughter."

–TIMOTHY WHITE
Catch a Fire: The Life of Bob Marley

IN TRUTH

"Rachel Carson brought to me the many voices of the ocean: its whispers and shouts, its whine, and its absolute silence. The sea is boundless in its mysteries. Those who never leave the edge of the sea may know little less than those who have voyaged across, or the diver who has touched the ocean floor. Reading *The Sea Around Us* took me ever closer to a feel for the workings of the ocean, its eternity, its nurturing of life."

–JEFFREY S. LEVINTON
from the afterword to Rachel L. Carson's *The Sea Around Us*

in·stinct

1.
*A powerful motivation
or impulse*

2.
*An innate capability or
aptitude*

3.
*An inborn pattern of
behavior that is
characteristic of a
species*

voice

1.
*Musical sound produced
by vibration of the
human vocal cords and
resonated within the
throat and head
cavities*

2.
Expression, utterance

3.
*The right or opportunity
to express an opinion;
a judgment; a vote*

words

1.
*Discourse or talk;
speech: to express*

2.
*An assurance or promise;
sworn intention*

2.
*Language that is spoken
or written*

CHAPTER 6

A LEADER BECOMES A LEADER
STANDING ALONE

"A small body of determined spirits fired by an
unquenchable faith in their mission
can alter the course of history."

—MOHANDAS GANDHI
freedom fighter in India and South Africa

STANDING ALONE

The difference between being a man alone on a launch pad in Cape Canaveral, Florida, and being the first man in history to set foot on the moon, was a 363-foot rocket called Apollo 11, and the courage of a pioneering astronaut named Neil Armstrong.

The difference between a man playing major league baseball in 1947, and a man standing alone as the first African-American to play in the major leagues, was Jackie Robinson's desire to sign with the Brooklyn Dodgers. His pioneering decision, and the vision of team general manager Branch Rickey, opened the door for players such as Willie Mays, Hank Aaron, and Roberto Clemente.

There are moments when only a handful of leaders are willing to take a stand, because the risks are so great that even the most powerful of purposes cannot overwhelm the natural human fear of failing. In these moments, risk and opportunity collide in a mysterious play in which enormous change and transformation are possible, but where most find a reason not to persevere.

The dangers of standing alone can be formidable. Neil Armstrong and the crew of Apollo 11 depended on a spacecraft made of fifteen million parts to hang together as they hurtled through space against physical forces that no one had ever experienced. The owners of the Dodgers warned Jackie Robinson that, as the first African-American to play in the major leagues, he'd be reviled, spat on, and sent death threats. And he was.

Robinson recalled of his momentous experience: "I had to fight hard against loneliness, abuse, and the knowledge that any mistake I made would be magnified because I was the only black man out there. Many people resented my impatience and honesty, but I never cared about acceptance as much as I cared about respect." Bill Anders, a pioneering astronaut from NASA's early Apollo program, evaluated the odds against the Apollo 11 astronauts this way: "I thought [Apollo 11] had one chance in three of a successful mission, one chance in three of an unsuccessful mission yet surviving, and one chance in three of an unsuccessful mission and not surviving."

And still, they stood. On April 15th, 1947, Jackie Robinson first set foot in the batter's box at Ebbetts Field in Brooklyn, New York. On July 20, 1969, Neil Armstrong's left foot touched on an unearthly dust that was the surface of the moon.

In Tiananmen Square, China, deep inside the walls of the glorious former Forbidden City, nearly one million student protesters and freedom fighters took control of the city center for a seven-week protest in the summer of 1989. There, in the midst of a grand and ancient civilization, they forged a powerful human wave of resistance against political oppression. When the government decided to clamp down, its army rolled a battery of tanks into the city to quell the protest and put an end to the embarrassing display of civil disobedience in a place built on order and deference to authority. The military killed hundreds of people that morning; many were shot in the back as they desperately tried to get away.

In the morning sun, a young man on the Avenue of Eternal Peace–it is believed that he was a nineteen-year-old student–walked out in front of the phalanx, quietly inquiring with his very presence as to why the authorities had chosen violence.

The quiet individual's action would halt eighteen tanks the size of small buildings. His presence would radiate from that place around the world–first across the city of Beijing, and then into the homes of people in every country with access to television. All the world instantly recognized in that broadcast image the meaning of being vulnerable and human, and standing up in the face of raw force. *Time* magazine would say of him: "The man who stood before the tanks reminded us that the conviction of the young can generate a courage that their elders sometimes lack." The article continued: "The image of the man before the tank stands for the [message]…that in a world ever more connected, the actions of a regular individual can light up the whole globe in an instant."

Reflecting on the power of Jackie Robinson's life, Elston Howard, a former catcher for the New York Yankees, explained what one leader standing alone can mean to so many others: "He meant everything to a black ballplayer…. I don't think the young players would go through what he did. He did it for all of us, for Willie Mays, Henry Aaron, Maury Wills, myself." Scott Simon would magnify Howard's perspective in his important book, *Jackie Robinson and the Integration of Baseball:* "He became the emblem of bearing up under great pressure and extraordinary circumstance for millions of Americans. Jackie Robinson not only changed the game of baseball, he changed the country that nourishes baseball."

Standing there, solitary, these leaders act as mother eagles, teaching their young to fly. Buzz Aldrin, Neil Armstrong's copilot from Apollo 11, said of the crew's leadership, "Just so much can be done on a formal team. A vast amount of preparation for life must be done on an individual basis." As their lunar module descended toward the moon's surface, and was running out of fuel seconds from the most important landing in human history, it must have seemed an impossible dream that they would report back to base camp minutes later, "Houston, Tranquility Base here. The Eagle has landed."

THE RESISTANCE OF
THE UNKNOWN REBEL
6.05.1989

"You gain strength, courage, and confidence by every experience
in which you really stop to look fear in the face. You are able to say to yourself,
I lived through this horror. I can take the next thing that comes along."

—ELEANOR ROOSEVELT
First Lady and social activist

The Unknown Rebel became a leader,
emerging from the shadows to stop an army.

STANDING ALONE

He stood on the Avenue of Eternal Peace near China's Tiananmen Square on June 5th, 1989. He stood in the shadows of the Gates of Heavenly Peace, a monument built six hundred years before to honor the ideals of unity and honor on which the Chinese people had built a great civilization.

HE STOOD FOR THE POWER OF THE INDIVIDUAL

Two days before, in Beijing, the Chinese government had unleashed tanks on its own citizens in Tiananmen Square, where a crowd a million strong–students, teachers, everyday citizens–had gathered for six long weeks to protest in support of the rights to free speech and greater personal freedom. Government officials, fed up with the growing unrest, sent the army in to quash the protest. After the troops killed hundreds and rid the streets of all the protesters, the lone dissenter walked out of the shadows.

His mere presence that day was subversive to the status quo. That a man would stand out in this way–rebellious and alone– and face down a phalanx of tanks spoke volumes about the changes that were at hand for an ancient society.

He wasn't an army general or a leading politician. He wasn't a revolutionary, a philosopher, or cutting-edge thinker. It is believed that the man who resisted the power of an army was a nineteen-year-old college student. He walked out from the anonymous crowd to stand in front of a line of tanks that towered above him like a city block of small buildings. He would stop the Chinese army that day, if only for a brief time. Television crews from around the world had gathered, and broadcast an image that riveted the world. It was instantly recognized for what it showed: an individual can take a stand, even in the face of overwhelming force, and make a difference.

This man, this student with his shopping bag, changed the course of history for a brief, shining moment. He demonstrated the power of peaceful resistance to every corner of the globe. The integrity of the man's spirit emitted an image so rich in human truth, and so undeniable in its meaning, that audiences everywhere could do nothing but stop and take notice.

Watch the event. There is a graceful moment when the student does a brief two-step with the tank operator who is leading the column. The tank motions to the right to test the student's resolve; the rebel moves to his left to stand again in front. The tank operator motions left; the student jumps to the right.

It is apparent that the tank operator wants nothing to do with the prospect of crushing a lone demonstrator. He nudges forward, and then stops. He nudges again. A military moment becomes an intimate human interaction, as two people thrust on center stage are each forced to decide what to do next. What has been a violent military action becomes a simple, small confrontation between one man trained to operate a tank weighing twenty-one tons, and another, with his shopping bag at his side, wondering if there aren't more reasonable ways for people to handle conflict.

It is said that there were two heroes that day: the anonymous individual who stood, and the tank operator who chose not to run him down. A third hero was the quiet, arresting spirit of peace that descended on a troubled city street to empower two brave souls to stop the violence, and negotiate together what to do next.

April 17th, 1989
At midnight on April 17th, a small group of Beijing University students gathers in Tiananmen Square in China to demonstrate support for grassroots political reform and free speech.

April 18th, 1989
In the first twenty-four hours, the protest attracts more than one thousand student protesters to the Square.

April 20th, 1989
Police and soldiers work to break up the crowd, beating and injuring hundreds of protesters.

April 27th, 1989
Students from more than forty Beijing college campuses join the burgeoning protest. The demonstration grows in just a few days to include more than one million people.

May 20th, 1989
The government of Premier Li Peng is stunned by the groundswell and declares martial law.

May 27th, 1989
Six weeks after the protest's inception, the students' resources run dangerously low, and the once-focused gathering turns chaotic. Health conditions and the imminent government clampdown cause the student leaders to announce that they will end the demonstration on May 30th.

May 27th to May 30th, 1989
Student representatives vote overwhelmingly to continue the protest, despite their leadership's concerns.

June 3rd, 1989
Troops and tanks begin to move on the center of the city. Soldiers randomly fire on the crowd, and tanks crush protesters. One frustrated participant cries, "You students can talk about nonviolence all you want, but our brothers and sisters have been killed."

June 5th, 1989
After the massacre, with hundreds of protesters dead and the streets of the city empty, a nineteen-year-old student wanders out of the shadows to stop the movement of an approaching column of tanks. Overwhelming force freezes in its tracks, as one citizen survives to question, "Why?" The image is broadcast worldwide and crystallizes the drama of Tiananmen Square.

June to December, 1989
The government of China posts a "Most Wanted List," and arrests protesters from around the country.

After December, 1989
The image of the student confronting the column of tanks becomes an international symbol for the power of individual integrity– one person standing up to overwhelming force.

The New York Times explained, "The television pictures of the incident, shown on the network news the same day it occurred, had an emotional immediacy that still burns in the mind."

THE FORBEARANCE OF
JACKIE ROBINSON

"A life is not important,
except in the impact it has on other lives."

–JACKIE ROBINSON
first African-American major league baseball player

Jackie Robinson became a leader, tolerating the worst in people
to open doors for thousands who followed him.

STANDING ALONE

Millions of young people dream of one day playing professional baseball in the major leagues. The odds against making it are staggering. One in fifty thousand high school athletes succeeds in becoming a professional athlete. In professional baseball, only ten percent of those fortunate enough to sign a major league contract ever actually play in a major league game.

HE MADE FORBEARANCE A MAJOR LEAGUE TRADEMARK

Jackie Robinson was one of those young people who thought he could beat the odds. Growing up a teenager in America in the 1930s, Robinson would flash his winning smile and baseball graces on diamonds around his neighborhood. To all onlookers, here was a young man who could clearly be one of the great baseball players.

But for Jackie Robinson, the odds of reaching the major leagues were not one in fifty thousand; they were essentially zero. "Ain't no colored players," the great Hank Aaron's father explained to his son. It was common wisdom among African-American families that their children would never make it to the major leagues. It was a time when people of color were not welcome at the table in a racially segregated society.

Against all odds, Jackie Robinson persevered. He made history by becoming the first African-American athlete to play major league baseball in the United States when he joined the Brooklyn Dodgers in 1947.

When the Dodgers recruited him, the team told him he would have to put up with the worst forms of derision. They explained the level of rage there would be, and the kind of invective and physical abuse that he would have to endure–all of which came true. Fans everywhere jeered at him, spit at him, and threw things. Even his own teammates signed a letter of protest, hoping to remove him from the team. But Robinson continued to beat the odds, demonstrating a capacity for forbearance that still amazes people today.

Despite the grueling circumstances, he would play with a brilliance that would lead to a lifetime batting average of .311, and a total of 197 stolen bases. At the end of an illustrious career, Robinson was inducted into Baseball's Hall of Fame in Cooperstown, New York. The induction marked the culmination of his baseball life, and proved a beacon of hope for athletes of color in a variety of sports around the world.

Bill Russell, the great NBA basketball player and another Hall of Famer, said that he might not have become a professional basketball player if Jackie Robinson had not first lit the path. Monte Irvin, another early black player who played for the New York Giants at the same time as Robinson, explained: "Jack was the trail-blazer, and we are all deeply grateful. We say, 'Thank you, Jackie; it was a job well done.'"

Hank Aaron, for decades major league baseball's all-time home run king, reflected in *Time* magazine on Robinson's monumental personal achievement: "To this day, I don't know how he withstood the things he did without lashing back. I've been through a lot in my time ... but I know I couldn't have done what Jackie did.... It was an incredible act of selflessness that brought the races...together...and shaped the dreams of an entire generation." Frank Robinson, the first African-American manager in the major leagues, went on to say, "By...walking among them, and showing everyone we could keep our heads high, he helped bring our whole society together."

1919
Jack Roosevelt Robinson is born to Jerry and Mallie Robinson in rural Cairo, Georgia. His grandfather was a slave. Both his parents are working sharecroppers.

1924-1933
Jackie, the youngest of five, grows up without his father (who left the family at an early age), but he is very close to his mother. Robinson writes of her in his autobiography, *I Never Had It Made*: "I thought she must have some kind of magic to be able to do all the things she did, to work hard and never complain and to make us all feel happy."

1936
Older brother Mack wins a silver medal at the Olympic Games in Berlin, Germany, finishing second to Jesse Owens in the two hundred meter sprint. Jackie reveres his brother and chooses to emulate his hard work and athleticism.

1940-1941
Robinson attends UCLA. He meets his beloved Rachel there, and becomes the first athlete in the school's history to letter in four sports in the same year.

1942
Robinson joins the U.S. Army during World War II, and rises to the rank of second lieutenant. He is court-martialed for not agreeing to sit in the back of a segregated military bus. After a fierce battle in which Robinson plays a critical role in defending himself, he is later acquitted and honorably discharged.

1947
Jackie Robinson signs with the Brooklyn Dodgers, and becomes the first African-American to play for a major league baseball team. With a signature, he sets the stage for the end of discrimination against black players. A sportswriter predicts that he has a "1,000-to-1 shot to make the grade." In his first year, Jackie becomes major league baseball's Rookie of the Year.

1947-1956
The Brooklyn Dodgers win six pennants in ten years with Robinson at shortstop.

1956
Jackie Robinson retires from baseball at age thirty-seven with a lifetime batting average of .311. He is voted into the Baseball Hall of Fame in Cooperstown, New York, in 1962, his first year of eligibility.

1957
Robinson becomes a business executive, and an active supporter of the civil rights movement.

1969
Robinson is invited to play in an Old Timer's game at Yankee Stadium, but refuses to participate to protest major league baseball's refusal to hire African-Americans as coaches or managers.

1972
Robinson makes his last public appearance at a World Series game at Riverfront Stadium in Cincinnati, and dies nine days later, on October 24th, of a heart attack, at fifty-three. He lives on as a symbol of courage and hope for people battling repression and inequality.

GLIMPSES OF YOUTH

Jackie letters in four sports during his storied collegiate athletic career at the University of California at Los Angeles.

1930-

"As time has passed, I've come to understand that the true value of Apollo wasn't the rocks, wasn't the data that we brought back. It was the worldwide sense of participation, of people everywhere recalling where they were at that moment, and how they shared in a human adventure that brought out the best in all of us."

—NEIL ARMSTRONG
first man to walk on the moon

Neil Armstrong became a leader in space thanks to his unusual capacity for grace under pressure

STANDING ALONE

Three-quarters of a billion people watched him take a walk. A third of a million people spent nearly a decade developing the technology and the fifteen million parts necessary to get him to the edge of the known world. Neil Armstrong opened a hatch on history some two hundred forty thousand miles from his home. He climbed out of the Eagle lunar landing module on July 24th, 1969, to tempt the unknown, alone on the surface of the moon for the very first time.

THE QUIET HUMILITY OF NEIL ARMSTRONG

It began when a dashing young president of the United States challenged a nation to touch the heavens. In 1963, John F. Kennedy brashly asserted: "I believe that this nation should commit itself to achieving the goal before this decade is out of landing a man on the moon and returning him safely to Earth."

The man who would lead that mission, Neil Armstrong, grew up in a small town in Ohio, an unassuming Eagle scout who impressed his teachers with his thorough and meticulous preparation. He was a boy obsessed with flying–a voracious reader of books about airplanes, a builder of models, a student pilot at just sixteen. He became a twenty-year-old top gun who could pilot a plane taking off catapulted from an aircraft carrier–one of the most difficult and feared maneuvers in the discipline of aviation.

He encountered his share of terror, from losing a wing in combat over Korea, to ejecting from a failed lunar launch trainer in 1968 just before it crashed and burned. Extreme risk was a constant cabin mate throughout his years of flying. And the mission to the first moon walk was no less harrowing. As the Eagle lunar lander made its final descent to the moon's surface, Armstrong, as commander of Apollo 11, realized that following the computer-generated path would land the Eagle and its crew in a rubble-strewn, treacherous crater. Simultaneously, Armstrong's copilot, Buzz Aldrin, ominously reported back to Houston, "Quantity light!" Which meant, in layman's terms, "We're running out of gas!" They had 114 seconds of fuel left to reach the surface, and sixty seconds to decide whether to abort the mission and return to the mother ship. Armstrong decided to continue, and manually pulled the craft out of its flight trajectory to find a stable place to land. The Eagle would touch down with forty seconds of descent fuel remaining. "The touchdown," Armstrong reflected after the mission, "was a real high in terms of elation. Not so much for the instant, but because it marked the achievement that a third of a million people had been waiting a decade to accomplish."

His wife, Linda, rooted him on from her television perch back on Earth as he started his now world-famous walk. "Be descriptive now, Neil," she urged under her breath, and her normally reticent husband seemed to transform as he took humankind's first walk on the surface. He rhapsodized with elation as he went, uncorking unexpected and unrehearsed peals of joy: "It has a stark beauty all its own," he rejoiced. "It's like much of the high desert of the United States."

Apollo 11's triumph has gone down as a touchstone moment in the history of our collective efforts to understand the world around us. Many historians believe that when most of the details of the past millennium have faded, Armstrong's walk will stand as the highest pinnacle in the history of human exploration. His left boot first touching the surface instantly changed him from a quiet pioneer to the most known and respected human on the planet. His response to the majestic triumph, and to the world's elation afterwards, was business as usual, an Armstrong trademark. While the world exploded with accolades on the crew's return, he walked back into the lives of his family and friends the same steady, quiet hero he had always been. It was as if fate had chosen him to be the first to take those historic steps, not just for his capacities to accomplish at the edges of what the human race had imagined possible, but for his natural abilities to preserve the nobility and magnificence of the journey. The deep, abiding dignity of the event has endured since. The heavenly potentials that exist above the horizon, and in the hearts of adventurers like Armstrong, beckon us on.

1930
Neil Armstrong is born on August 5th, on his grandparents' farm in Wapakoneta, Ohio.

1933-1945
Two-year-old Neil sees his first airplane. At six, he takes his first flight. As a child, he becomes an inveterate model airplane builder, and spends his free time chasing down new magazines about flight. He works as a mechanic at the local airfield to save enough money to eventually take flying lessons.

1946
When he is fifteen, Armstrong regularly visits neighbor Jacob Zint's backyard to peer through his telescope at the Sea of Tranquility, the site on the moon he will eventually visit.

1950
Armstrong enters the Korean War as a Navy pilot during his sophomore year in college, and flies seventy-eight combat missions.

1962
After working seven years as a civilian test pilot, Armstrong joins the élite corps of astronauts in the U.S. space flight group.

1966
As commander of Gemini 8, Armstrong is forced to abandon what is planned to be a three-day space flight when a short-circuit in the craft's systems disables the ship's thrusters.

1968
NASA chooses Neil Armstrong to command Apollo 11, the historic space mission during which the first human being would walk on the moon. "I wasn't chosen to be [the] first [to walk]," he would say. "I was just chosen to command that flight."

July 18th, 1969
"Deke" Slayton, the NASA chief overseeing the Apollo mission, explains the planning process: "There isn't any big, magic selection that goes on.... You've got a mission to do...and you assign guys to fly them. It's that straightforward."

July 24th, 1969
As commander of Apollo 11, thirty-eight-year-old Neil Armstrong climbs down the steps of the Eagle lunar landing module and walks on the moon for the first time in human history. He says, "That's one small step for a man, one giant leap for mankind."

1971
Armstrong resigns from NASA.

2007
Armstrong has been honored by seventeen countries around the world. He is a successful business executive, devoting his energies to several aviation businesses.

When Neil Armstrong was just sixteen, he received a pilot's license– well before he even had a license to drive an automobile.

virtues OF LEADERSHIP

"Almost nobody knew his name. Nobody outside his immediate neighborhood had read his words or heard him speak. Nobody knows what happened to him even one hour after his moment in the world's living rooms. But the man who stood before a column of tanks near Tiananmen Square–June 5, 1989–may have impressed his image on the global memory more vividly, more intimately than even Sun Yat-sen did. Almost certainly he was seen in his moment of self-transcendence by more people than ever laid eyes on Winston Churchill, Albert Einstein, and James Joyce combined.

The meaning of his moment–it was no more than that– was instantly decipherable in any tongue, to any age: even the billions who cannot read…could follow what the 'tank man' did…. One lone Everyman standing up to machinery, to force."

−*TIME* MAGAZINE
"The Unknown Rebel"

"A second baseman is in a highly vulnerable position. In making the pivot on the double play, he generally has his back to the runner, who attempts to prevent the fielder from completing the throw to first base. In this situation baserunners unleashed their aggressions against Robinson. 'I've seen the time when if it'd been me, well, the fight would've started,' recalls Tatum. Robinson, however, usually went out of his way to stress that the rough-and-tumble play at second base was a part of the game. After one incident in which Robinson had to be helped from the field, he defended the baserunner. 'He didn't rough me up,' said Robinson. 'He only came in hard and fast. That's the way to play baseball.'"

−JULES TYGIEL
Baseball's Great Experiment: Jackie Robinson and His Legacy

STANDING ALONE

"From the very first days, when man sought to master the unknown by finding out what the valley next to his was like, until today, when the unknown is the solar system, man has had to conquer the fear of the dangers which the unknown conceals, not only as they are but as he fancies them. The companions of Barholomeu Diaz had to conquer the fear that the ocean at and beyond the equator might boil or drop into a cosmic precipice; the companions of Columbus feared griffins, sirens, men with tails or with their heads screwed to their navels. Our astronauts' imagination is more disciplined by knowledge, but even in our day, when fancy and imagination have been disposed of, what remains is forbidding enough. Yet man is not daunted. These undaunted men are the true creators of history, those thanks to whom history is not a blind chain of facts but a clear-sighted sequence of acts–events that were ideas before they happened. It is from men who act on nature, and do not merely suffer to be acted upon by her, that history flows."

−SALVADOR DE MARDARIAGA
Spanish-born historian and philosopher, expert on the voyages of Columbus,
"A New World: Moon Supplement," *Time* magazine

re·sis·tance

1.
The action of opposing something with which you disapprove or disagree

2.
Opposition, passive or active

for·bear·ance

1.
Tolerance and restraint in the face of provocation

2.
The exercise of patience

3.
Good-natured tolerance

hu·mil·i·ty

1.
The quality or condition of being humble

2.
Freedom from pride and arrogance

CHAPTER 7

A LEADER BECOMES A LEADER
SOWING PEACE

"Hatred does not cease by hatred at any time,
but hatred ceases by love; this is an eternal truth."

–GAUTAMA BUDDHA
enlightened holy man

SOWING PEACE

"Peace is not the product of terror or fear. Peace is not the silence of cemeteries. Peace is not the silent result of violent repression. Peace is the generous, tranquil contribution of all to the good of all. Peace is dynamism. Peace is generosity. It is right and it is duty." The words poured naturally from a man who spent his days seeking peace in one of the most violent places in the world. He worked shoulder to shoulder with the poorest members of his country, fighting so that their voices could be heard in a place that was languishing in acute and widespread poverty. He spoke passionately for social reform as death squads roamed the neighborhoods, imposing their own radical order at the end of the barrel of a gun, and from the heart of an anonymous darkness.

Assassins would take the life of Salvadoran archbishop Oscar Romero, but his commitment to people living by high ideals and core principles such as nonviolence, despite desperate oppression, lives on in the hearts and minds of the people he touched.

Nelson Mandela, Mohandas Gandhi, and Aung San Suu Kyi became leaders in places equally fraught with chaos and oppression, where governments had stripped the people of basic human rights and freedoms. These leaders came to serve in places where the only reasonable response to the status quo was violence, retaliation, and war. And still, they made it their duty to contribute broadly and generously to the spirit and the good of all through self-sacrifice, risk, and steady forbearance.

Gandhi explained the challenge this way: "The virtues of mercy, nonviolence, love, and truth in any man can be tested only when they are pitted against ruthlessness, violence, hate, and untruth." He would also write: "Nonviolence in its dynamic condition means conscious suffering. It does not mean meek submission to the will of the evil doer, but it means the pitting of one's whole soul against the will of the tyrant."

Aung San Suu Kyi, the leader of the freedom movement in Burma, a country of forty-six million people enslaved by a military junta since 1962, explained her countrymen's turmoil this way: "I ask people why they want democracy. Very often the answer is, 'We just want to be free.' They do not have to elaborate....

They want to be able to live their lives without the oppressive sense that their destiny is not theirs to shape. They do not want their daily existence to be ruled by the orders and whims of those whose authority is based on might of arms."

As a symbol of freedom and conscience to millions of people, she has for years tolerated jail and painful separation from her family to shine the bright spotlight of world attention on an unbearable situation. Lives of leaders like Aung San Suu Kyi suggest that there is an art to sowing peace. We hear in their stories the sounds of resolute courage, of patience in the face of atrocities, of nonviolence as a reaction to the worst human horrors. They sow peace in places where vast and bitter conflict reign. They lift spirits where dark political oppression robs people of their dreams and their freedom. They are not passive or detached, but engaged in carefully constructed opposition.

They are ordinary people who align with the best of the human spirit, and draw from the well of ideals a new way to lead. Nelson Mandela described his role in the evolution of South Africa, where he sought change from prison for twenty-seven years: "I was not a messiah, but an ordinary man who had become a leader because of extraordinary circumstances." *Time* magazine would amplify: "Mandela prove[d] through his own example that faith, hope, and charity are qualities attainable by humanity as a whole. Through his willingness to walk the road of sacrifice, he has reaffirmed our common potential to move toward a new age."

Mohandas Gandhi was the leader of India's freedom fight, and a fierce adherent to nonviolent methods of resolving conflict. The famous photograph of this solitary man working steadily at his spinning wheel shines out from history like a beacon, inviting those who follow him to be equally self-determined, free from complications, and at peace. Gandhi's successor in India, Jawarharlal Nehru, watched this man–whom many around the world have come to revere as one of the great leaders of modern times–move to an important political demonstration: "As I saw him marching, staff in hand, to Dandi on the Salt March in 1930…[h]ere was the pilgrim on his quest of truth, quiet, peaceful, determined and fearless, who could continue that quest and pilgrimage, regardless of consequences."

"I am sure love and compassion will triumph in the end."

–AUNG SAN SUU KYI
leader of the Burmese freedom fight

Aung San Suu Kyi became a leader for freedom,
maintaining perspective in the worst set of circumstances.

SOWING PEACE

She speaks to the free world about what it is like to live in an unfree society, because she knows how difficult it is for people living in relative peace and freedom to understand the suffering of people living under an authoritarian government. She stays in jail when she has to, because she knows that speaking her mind and her conscience brings her greater freedom than anything that exists for her on the outside.

SHE KINDLES THE LIGHT OF FREEDOM FOR MILLIONS OF FELLOW COUNTRYMEN

Her name is Aung San Suu Kyi, and she leads the freedom fight in Burma as head of the National League of Democracy. She knows what it is to live in slavery, as do millions of other Burmese people whom she represents in a fight to overthrow a tyrannical government that uses torture, brutality, and secrecy as weapons to protect the power, control, and wealth of a very few.

In Burma, young people are unable to gather, to discuss current events, to criticize the government, or to share openly ideas about how to improve society. The oppressive regime prohibits all the natural elements of a youth worth living–no trying out new styles and new moods, no creativity, no rebelliousness, no singing, no shouting, no dating, and no dancing.

Women struggle to manage the basic essentials of home life, oppressed by rapidly rising prices that make stability nearly impossible. Many turn to prostitution to help their families survive. Men isolate themselves, afraid of trying to better their circumstances, as any misperceived word or action may bring charges of treason, and a lengthy prison stay.

In their minds, it is better to suffer a slow mental and emotional death than to risk separation from a family that needs support and protection.

In the midst of the catastrophic darkness, the work of Aung San Suu Kyi and the other freedom fighters lights a candle to kindle the fading hope of millions of people. Through nonviolent but active resistance, she stands for freedom, giving the downtrodden a voice, and a glimpse of hope.

She gives them a voice through her voice, speaking out internationally about the atrocities being perpetrated in Burma. She gives them a glimpse of freedom, a freedom that is so out of sight it is hard for the Burmese even to imagine what it is any longer to be free. And she gives them a sense of hope, a hope that comes from a new, dynamic definition of freedom that allows the people to begin to rise, even as they languish in unspeakable conditions.

She calls it freedom of conscience. "As I travel through my country," she recently wrote in *Parade* magazine, "people often ask me how it feels to have been imprisoned in my home–first for six years–then for nineteen months. How could I stand the separation from family and friends? It is ironic, I say, that in an authoritarian state, it is only the prisoner of conscience who is genuinely free."

"The quest for democracy in Burma," she said in accepting the Nobel Peace Prize, "is the struggle of a people to live whole, meaningful lives as free and equal members of the world community. It is part of the unceasing human endeavor to prove that the spirit of man can transcend the flaws of his nature."

When the Nobel Committee granted her its highest honor, the chairman said of her: "With her courage and high ideals, Aung San Suu Kyi brings out something of the best in us…knowing she is there gives us faith in the power of good."

1945
Aung San Suu Kyi is born to General Aung San and Dawn Khin Kyi in Rangoon, the capital of Burma. Her father is the commander of the Burma Independence Army.

1947
Her father is assassinated when Suu Kyi is an infant. Her mother responds to his death by taking on an important role in Burmese politics.

1948
Burma becomes an independent nation as a result of the freedom fight.

1964-1967
Aung San Suu Kyi attends Oxford University, and receives her bachelor of arts in philosophy, politics and economics. She meets Michael Aris, a student of Asian civilization.

1972
Suu Kyi marries Michael Aris, and they settle in the Himalayas, where Aris works.

1973-1978
Aung San Suu Kyii becomes a mother of two boys, Alexander and Kim.

1984-1988
Suu Kyi becomes a published writer. Titles include *Let's Visit Burma*, a children's book, and *Aung San*. She continues her work in academia as a visiting scholar at the Southeast Asian Studies Center in Kyoto, Japan. Her father's leadership legacy remains a cornerstone of her academic interests.

1988
Aung San Suu Kyi enters the political arena for the first time. She addresses hundreds of thousands of people during the summer of 1988 at an outdoor rally, inspiring the crowd to call for democracy, and to push for freedom and change. The military regime clamps down further. Suu Kyi is elected general secretary of the newly created National League for Democracy, which is founded on principles of nonviolent and civil disobedience.

1990
Suu Kyi's National League for Democracy wins a landslide victory in the general election, but is prevented from assuming power.

1989-1995
Suu Kyi is placed under house arrest, and remains there for six years. She coauthors *Freedom from Fear* with her husband, Michael. The junta offers to release her if she will leave the country to live with her family. She refuses. She is honored with the Nobel Peace Prize in 1991.

1999
Her husband dies of prostate cancer after a four-year period in which he has petitioned the Burmese authorities in vain to allow him to enter the country and see his wife one last time.

2007
Suu Kyi remains under house arrest. She is a symbol of hope for millions of Burmese people enslaved by the military government.

Aung San Suu Kyi's father and eight of his political associates were assassinated when Suu Kyi was just two years old. She has since dedicated her life's work as a freedom fighter in Burma to his memory.

1918–

"A man who takes away another man's freedom is a prisoner of hatred, he is locked behind the bars of prejudice and narrow-mindedness…. For to be free is not merely to cast off one's chains, but to live in a way that respects and enhances the freedom of others."

—NELSON MANDELA
former president of South Africa

Nelson Mandela became a leader in South Africa trusting in the power of stillness to change the world

SOWING PEACE

He spent twenty-seven years in prison, surviving on broth and core principles, writing, meditating, watching, waiting, weathering, exercising, listening, planning with fellow inmates, negotiating with the South African authorities, knowing that he would stand vigil–a lifetime's vigil, if necessary–until all of the people of his country were free. The authorities told him that he could be released any day, at any time, if he would just renounce his dedication to the movement for democratic self-rule–the principle of "one man, one vote"–that had been prohibited in South Africa during the reign of apartheid.

THE STEADY DETERMINATION OF NELSON MANDELA

But Nelson Mandela would never renounce the cause–not even on pain of death would he renounce, he said–because to do so would have been to deny the very essence of what he had become. He wrote in his autobiography *Long Walk to Freedom*: "I had no epiphany, no singular revelation, no moment of truth; but a steady accumulation of a thousand slights, a thousand indignities, a thousand unremembered moments, that produced in me an anger, a rebelliousness, a desire to fight the system that imprisoned my people. There was no particular day on which I said, 'From henceforth I will devote myself to the liberation of my people'; instead, I simply found myself doing so, and could not do otherwise."

Through all the indignities, and the long years of injustice and imprisonment, he carried with him a steadfast dedication to principled behavior. With his colleagues, he treated the prison guards with respect and care despite the harshest treatment. Together he and his fellow prisoners sang African freedom songs from their prison cells into the heart of the loneliest nights. They set up an internal "university" to share expertise from prisoner to thought-starved prisoner.

The heroic moments that followed in the face of the worst human brutality collected like droplets of rain water. The raindrops spilled into waterways that slowly, steadily, over the expanse of years, carved a vibrant canyon of self-determination and freedom for the South African people. The government freed the prisoners, and unconditionally released Nelson Mandela on February 11th, 1990.

From overwhelming oppression and personal sacrifice would blossom some of the most glorious revelations for Nelson Mandela. The other prisoners committed to the freedom fight began, in Mandela's eyes, to glow in character, like chestnuts of dazzling precious metals, after the years of imprisonment and hard labor. Mandela's own language best honors the suffering and transformation of his fellow inmates: "The decades of brutality had another, unintended effect and that was that it produced the Oliver Tambos, the Walter Sisulus, the Chief Luthulis, the Yusuf Dedoos, the Bram Fischers, the Robert Sobukwes of our time–men of such extraordinary courage, wisdom and generosity that their like may never be known again. Perhaps it requires such depth of oppression to create such heights of character. My country is rich in the minerals and gems that lie beneath its soil, but I have always known that its greatest wealth is its people, finer and truer than the purest diamonds."

In the end, it wasn't just for the humanity of his comrades or for the humanity of his people that he was fighting. The magnificence of Nelson Mandela's story lies in the magnanimity and universality of his vision. Like the steady drops of rain that made the canyon of change possible, this man would stop at nothing to create a truly generous and free society.

"I knew as well as I knew anything that the oppressor must be liberated just as surely as the oppressed. A man who takes away another man's freedom is a prisoner of hatred, he is locked behind the bars of prejudice and narrow-mindedness.... For to be free is not merely to cast off one's chains, but to live in a way that respects and enhances the freedom of others. The true test of our devotion to freedom is just beginning."

1918
Rolihlahla Dalibhunga "Nelson" Mandela is born to Chief Henry and Nosekeni Mandela on the Eastern Cape of South Africa. He spends his childhood in the countryside, herding cattle and playing and stick-fighting with the other boys of the village. He begins to explore his people's mystical connection to the land and animals that surround his village.

1927
Mandela's father and mother are the family's anchors. His mother shares with her family legends and fables that capture "virtue and generosity" being "rewarded in ways that one cannot know." When he is nine, his father dies, and he becomes the ward of the acting regent of the Thembu people, Chief Jongintaba Dalindyebi, who raises him.

1935
Mandela becomes a student at the missionary College of Fort Hare, where he works with other student protesters to fight race-based colonial rule of the college. It is his first exposure to the oppressive system of apartheid, a political system that systematically disenfranchises citizens according to race.

1952
Mandela becomes the deputy president of the African National Congress, whose goal is to create a multiracial society.

1961
As a prominent member of the country's young resistance fighters, Mandela is indicted for high treason, along with one hundred fifty-five others. After a five-year trial, he and the others are acquitted of all charges.

1962
Mandela is convicted and sentenced to five years in jail for "endorsing an armed struggle." In 1963, already in jail, he is charged with attempting to overthrow the government, and is condemned to a life sentence.

1980
Oliver Tambo and the A.N.C. rally constituents from around the world in a "Release Mandela" campaign after he has spent eighteen years in jail.

1990
The new president of South Africa, F. W. de Klerk, frees all African citizens by ending opposition to the A.N.C and announcing that Nelson Mandela will be released from prison after twenty-seven years.

1998
Mandela explains his own position in history: "I was not a messiah, but an ordinary man who had become a leader because of extraordinary circumstances."

2007
Nelson Mandela becomes an international symbol of hope, wisdom, vision, patience, and moral integrity. His extraordinary personal sacrifice to free a people leaves a legacy of justice and decency that rings around the world.

Nelson Mandela was suspended from college soon after arriving for participating in a protest march.

"Become the change that you want to see in the world."

—MOHANDAS GANDHI
liberator, India and South Africa

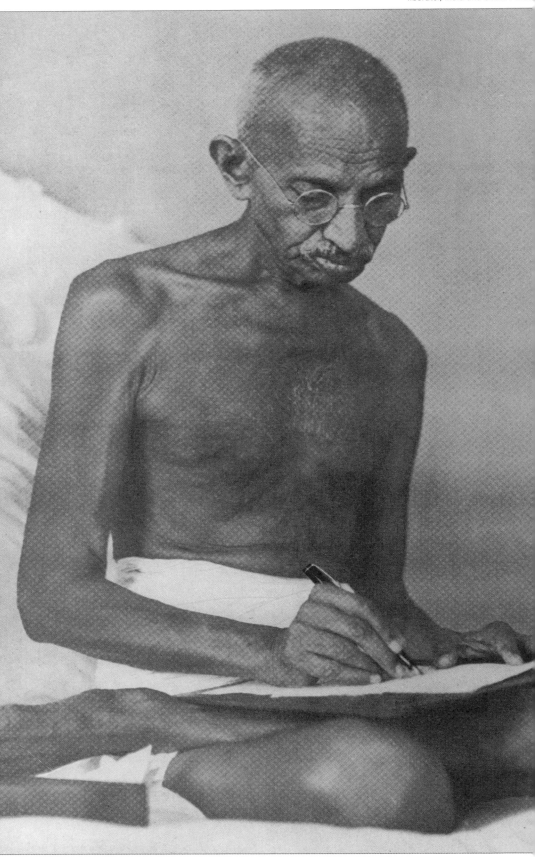

Mohandas Gandhi became a leader around the world
experimenting with truth and the essence of a human life

SOWING PEACE

Albert Einstein said of Mohandas Gandhi, "Generations to come will scarce believe that such a one as this ever… walked upon this earth." It is high praise from one of the most belief-shaking scientists the world has ever known. This Indian man, this mahatma (literally, "great soul"), who freed millions of people, and in his lifetime helped shape the spirit and principal tenets of leaders who came after him, such as Dr. Martin Luther King, Jr., and Nelson Mandela, was uncommon and unrelenting in his mission to advance the cause of human freedom and civilization.

HE EXPERIMENTED WITH THE POWER OF SIMPLE THINGS

In his biographical portrait of the man, *Mohandas Gandhi and His Disciples*, the Indian author Ved Mehta describes how unlikely this leader's rise to influence was: "Gandhi was not endowed with any unusual artistic, scholarly, or scientific talents. He never… received any special academic honors. He was never a candidate in an election or a holder of public office. Yet when he died in 1948, at the age of seventy-eight, practically the whole world would mourn him."

Why? Who was this humble man with those now-famous wire-rimmed spectacles who etched his thoughts onto a simple tablet, and spun thread quietly at his spinning wheel? Like Albert Einstein, Mohandas Gandhi was one of the great experimenters of his age. He titled his autobiography *The Story of My Experiments in Truth*, because for him, the energies of a human life were malleable and meant to be shaped and molded through experimentation and experience to support a high purpose and the betterment of all human life. This man of the people–he would free more than a billion people in his time–did not experiment with atoms, or test tubes, or with new postulates about the laws of physics. Instead, he experimented with the stuff of leadership, and with the stuff of a human life.

He began as the son of an Indian politician. He went on to study law. But when he famously encountered racial intolerance on a train trip in South Africa in 1893, he changed his life's direction, and dedicated himself to fighting oppression and intolerance wherever he encountered it. Authorities removed him from the train because of the color of his skin. "It was winter," Gandhi would write in his autobiography, "and the cold was extremely bitter. My overcoat was in my luggage, but I did not dare to ask for it lest I should be insulted again, so I sat and shivered."

From that train platform, he dedicated his life to ending a people's suffering. As a leader, he had the means to enjoy fine clothing, but he wore the garb of the poorest peasant, dressing more humbly than the people he had come to represent. Although he could have traveled in style, he traveled in third class, sitting on hard benches in very crowded quarters. From his eating habits, to his dress, to every facet of his life, Mohandas Gandhi worked to rid himself of worldly concerns, so that he could focus solely on the cause of freedom.

Gandhi once said, "As human beings, our greatness lies not so much in being able to remake the world–that is the myth of the atomic age–as in being able to remake ourselves." Mohandas Gandhi remade himself. From the heart of a simple life of experimentation would come the freedom of a billion people, first in South Africa and then in India.

Nelson Mandela, the president of South Africa, honored Gandhi's contributions in 1997, at the very train station where his life's mission began: "Gandhi's magnificent example of personal sacrifice and dedication in the face of oppression was one of his many legacies…. He showed us that it was necessary to brave imprisonment if truth and justice were to triumph over evil. The values of tolerance, mutual respect, and unity for which he stood and acted had a profound influence on our liberation movement, and on my own thinking." He left a life of ease to wander out among the maelstrom of human suffering, and bring peace and freedom to many corners. An assassin would take his life in 1948. The man approached Gandhi, saying, "You are late today, Mahatmaji." For the hundreds of millions that he worked to set free, Mohandas Gandhi's approach to leadership came just in time.

GANDHI'S LIFE

1869
Mohandas Karamchand Gandhi is born to Karamachand and Putilibai Gandhi in Porbandar, Gujarat India. His father is the former prime minister of the family's village; his mother is a devout woman, dedicated to the notion that one should respect all people, regardless of caste or cultural upbringing.

1874-1882
The young Gandhi is engaged to be married three times by the time he is seven. He is married at thirteen in a union that will last more than sixty years.

1888
While studying to become a lawyer in London, Gandhi privately studies two ancient spiritual texts—the Christian *Bible* and the Hindu *Bhagavad Gita*–from which he adopts two life principles. The first he calls Satyagraha, the force of truth and love. The second is Ahimsa, or nonviolence to all living things.

1893-1913
Gandhi is asked to practice law in South Africa. There, he commits himself to a struggle that will last some twenty years to free Indians and other people of color from a system of submission and repression.

1914
After a twenty-year struggle, marked by constant indignities and jail time, Gandhi achieves victory: South Africa eases its worst forms of institutionalized injustice against people of color. Gandhi returns to his native land to help free the people in India.

1915
At forty-five, Gandhi begins a thirty-year political struggle using his philosophy of nonviolence and civil disobedience to rid his homeland of its occupiers. More than thirty thousand people will be jailed in an unrelenting three decades of fierce confrontation.

1930
Gandhi organizes a march to the sea to demonstrate that his country can achieve self-determination.

1947
The occupiers relent, and allow India independence and self-rule. Although sectarian differences cause deep schisms in the country, Gandhi's vision of a freed people is realized.

1948
Mohandas Gandhi is killed by an assassin. His country reveres him as "Bapuji" or "Father of the Nation."

Admirers around the world will continue to believe that he is the symbolic father of a universal nation, to which everyone belongs, that celebrates greater justice, freedom, truth, and peace.

GLIMPSES OF YOUTH

Gandhi grew up afraid of many of the things in his world, including animals, darkness and ghosts. His thirteen-year-old wife helped him overcome his fears and gain confidence, although he remained afraid of the dark much of his life.

virtues
OF LEADERSHIP

"The quintessential revolution is that of the spirit.
It is not enough merely to call for freedom, democracy, and
human rights. There has to be a united determination to persevere
in the struggle, to make sacrifices in the name of enduring truths,
to resist the corrupting influences of desire,
ill will, ignorance, and fear."

—AUNG SAN SUU KYI
Freedom From Fear

"When the apartheid regime sent Nelson Mandela to prison
for life back in 1962, they thought they had silenced a powerful voice for freedom.
But how wrong they were. No chains, no iron bars could still the revolutionary
spirit of Nelson Mandela and his courageous colleagues in the African National
Congress. When he was sentenced to life imprisonment, he concluded his speech
to the Court with a soul-stirring vision…. And he said, 'During my lifetime, I
have cherished the ideal of a democratic society in which all persons live together
in harmony and with equal opportunities. It is an ideal which I hope to live for
and to achieve but if need be it is an ideal for which I am prepared to die.'…
When he emerged from twenty-seven years of prison,… Nelson Mandela captured
the imagination of the world with his unyielding pride, his remarkable lack of bit-
terness, and most of all his uncompromising principles and
vigorous commitment to the struggle against apartheid."

—CORETTA SCOTT KING
from *The Eyes on the Prize: Civil Rights Reader: Documents, Speeches, and
Firsthand Accounts from the Black Freedom Struggle, 1954-1990,* by Clayborne Carson

SOWING PEACE

"Gandhi's experiments were leading him
into rarely traveled regions deep below the surface level of living,
where the ordinary values of buying and selling, prestige and pleasure,
held no meaning at all. Writers and philosophers before him had written
thick volumes on truth and happiness, but few of them had been able
to change their lives. Gandhi was not interested in such abstract principles.
He wanted to know how to live, and was willing to transform his whole
personality, if necessary, to bring him closer to that goal. He scrutinized the
lives and works of men from many other nationalities and faiths,
looking for a guide. When he found one at last it was in
the spiritual tradition of his land, a tradition unbroken
for more than five thousand years."

—EKNATH EASWARAN
Gandhi The Man: The Story of His Transformation

free·dom

1.
Liberty; independence

2.
Exemption from the power and control of another

3.
The capacity to exercise choice; free will

de·ter·mi·na·tion

1.
Firmness of purpose; resolve; a fixed intention or resolution

2.
The quality of mind which reaches definite conclusions; decisiveness of character

ex·per·i·men·ta·tion

1.
The testing of an idea

2.
An innovative act or procedure

3.
To try something new, especially in order to gain experience

CHAPTER 8

A LEADER BECOMES A LEADER
SEEKING JUSTICE

"Cowardice asks the question, 'Is it safe?'
Expediency asks the question, 'Is it politic?'
Vanity asks the question, 'Is it popular?'
But conscience asks the question, 'Is it right?' And
there comes a time that one must take a position that
is neither safe, nor politic, nor popular, but one must
take it, because one's conscience tells one
that it is right."

–MARTIN LUTHER KING, JR.
January 10th, 1959

A LEADER BECOMES A LEADER
SEEKING JUSTICE

Eleanor Roosevelt, probably the most significant social activist of the first half of the twentieth century, said, "In the long run, we shape our lives and we shape ourselves.... And the choices we make are ultimately our responsibility."

She was a woman who spent the better part of a lifetime lobbying the most powerful to pay attention to the needs of the weakest, a woman of means and power who chose to step outside the circumstances of her comfortable life to address the desperate needs of people living in chronic poverty. It was through the pursuit of her vision of a more balanced and fair society that she would become one of the most outspoken champions of civil rights in her day, and in so doing, propel the world forward in a quest for decency.

"Where, after all, do universal human rights begin?" she wrote. "In small places, close to home–so close and so small that they cannot be seen on any maps of the world. Yet they are the world of the individual person: the neighborhood he lives in; the school or college he attends; the factory, farm, or office where he works. Such are the places where every man, woman, and child seeks equal justice.... Unless these rights have meaning there, they have little meaning anywhere. Without concerted citizen action to uphold them close to home, we shall look in vain for progress in the larger world."

Leaders such as Eleanor Roosevelt cannot guarantee that justice will render tidy reckonings. There is no measuring its reach, or understanding where it begins, or determining where we are on its mighty and expansive continuum.

But you know it when a leader makes justice a vital priority in her work. You know when justice rules in the hearts of people. You know when it changes a society. You know it when it arrives unexpectedly on life's branch like a mockingbird to influence the very timbre of a person's life. And you know when justice is lost, and people suffer.

A little black girl's parents choose to send their daughter to an elementary school that has never been integrated. Every day, the six-year-old must face an ugly gauntlet of vicious protesters just to get inside the school. But, nevertheless, she walks into the history of the civil rights movement as she goes up the front steps accompanied by federal marshals, trailed by an onslaught of hate and fear from a time that is being left behind. A woman in the crowd screams that she wants to poison the little girl. A young boy holds up a mock casket with a little black doll inside, terrifying her and causing her to wonder if she should ever come to school again. She cracks the concrete block walls of racial prejudice at the school one small chip at a time, not with a hammer, but with a small girl's resolve, deliberate energy, and steady heart.

A young, vibrant man chooses to let the world know who he is, and in so doing, faces the threat of assassination. He is fed up with a hidden life, with the strange and horrifying realization he first had as a teenager that the more he becomes who he is, the more society will ostracize him. He chooses to reveal first to his friends, then to his family, and then to society, that he is a gay man. He will become an important politician, and make civil rights for gay people a paramount item on the agenda. Because of his courage, a city will begin the long process of healing. Eventually, gay people will stop fearing that they will be brutalized around the next corner, lose their jobs, or become a statistic on a city's homicide ledger simply because of who they are. His words and actions will unleash a new wave of justice and decency.

We hear the distant trains. Their tracks lead from the sources of human hope, into places where fairness can sometimes prevail, but where circumstances often overwhelm the light of justice and allow darkness in for another day. Mohandas Gandhi, the great freedom fighter of South Africa and India, explained that victory for him was the simple existence of the struggle itself, and that any small movements toward a fairer society, regardless of the strength of the resistance, are enough to make an activist sleep well at night.

In the Academy Award-winning film of Harper Lee's novel, *To Kill a Mockingbird*, a country lawyer, Atticus Finch, is trying to save the life of an innocent man. This character, who has become the embodiment of what it means to be a champion of justice, explains: "Before I can live with other folks, I've got to live with myself. The one thing that doesn't abide by majority rule is a person's conscience."

"I do hope that I have inspired some of you today to join me again by dedicating yourselves to not just protecting but uplifting those you touch, because that will enable us to rise together as a people, as a nation, and as a world."

—RUBY BRIDGES HALL
founder, Ruby Bridges Foundation

Ruby Bridges became a leader in grade school because she was willing to stand for justice no matter what the cost.

SEEKING JUSTICE

Imagine four armed federal marshals arriving early in the morning at a little girl's home in New Orleans to escort her and her mother through the streets of her hometown in a police vehicle to the local elementary school.

THEY CALLED HER THE 'CLASS OF ONE'

Now imagine a different band of federal marshals taking positions around the building to contain the gathered crowd, and to suppress potential outbreaks of violence, as the girl and her mother approach the school to enter for the very first time.

It happened on the morning of November 14th, 1960.

Ruby Bridges, at just six years old, became the first child of color to enter what would be the first racially integrated public school in New Orleans, Louisiana. It was called the William Frantz Elementary School.

In the fall of 1960, federal district judge J. Skelly Wright ordered schools in New Orleans to integrate, and to accept African-American students for the first time in the city's history. It was a landmark court decision for a Southern culture and establishment that had resisted equality for African-Americans through the violent conflagration of the Civil War and the everyday violence and oppression that followed. Up until then, the school system's policy of "separate but equal" maintained segregated schools as the status quo.

It was a terrifying scene as the little girl arrived at the elementary school that morning. Adults jeered and spewed hate. Children protested loudly. One grown woman threatened to poison her. Placards, crosses, and signs filled the crowded space around her as she walked up the sidewalk and into the school. Families kept their children away to protest what the judge had decided.

But Ruby Bridges came anyway. She came, and, as a "class of one," walked into the school past all the angry people. She walked past the jeers, past the hate, and into the history books as a child who helped break down the barriers to fairness for millions of children who would eventually follow her through the door that she opened that first morning.

Barbara Henry was her teacher that first year at the William Frantz School. She was a healing presence who supported the six-year-old's resolve, and who made her stay at the school bearable. Despite the potential danger, Ruby Bridges came to that school, and to Barbara Henry's empty classroom, day after day, enduring the hostility until, finally, it began to dissipate, as a city came to terms with its newfound approach to education.

One morning, as the threats raged, Barbara Henry watched Ruby from the classroom window as she talked to the mob while walking into the building. She was surprised that the girl would talk to the angry crowd. "I saw your lips moving," she said, "but I couldn't make out what you were saying to those people."

"I wasn't talking to them," Ruby answered. "I was praying for them."

RUBY'S LIFE

1951
Oliver Brown, an African-American minister and railroad welder, sues the Topeka, Kansas, Board of Education, asserting that, by not allowing his daughter to attend a school near her home because of her race, it is violating certain basic rights guaranteed under the Constitution of the United States.

1954
Three years after Brown's lawsuit, the Supreme Court rules unanimously that segregation violates the Fourteenth Amendment of the Constitution, which guarantees all citizens equal protection under the law. Ruby Bridges is born to Abon and Lucille Bridges in Tylertown, Mississippi.

1960
The National Association for the Advancement of Colored People contacts Ruby Bridges's parents to let them know that their daughter has been chosen to be one of the first African-American children to attend an integrated elementary school. Escorted by an entourage of four federal marshals on the morning of November 14th, six-year-old Ruby becomes the first African-American child to attend what had been an all-white elementary school in New Orleans, Louisiana.

Militant segregationists surround the school to block her entry. Charles Burk, one of the escorting marshals, would later remember Ruby's poise and heroism: "She showed a lot of courage.... She just marched along like a little soldier."

Ruby becomes a class of one, as no other parents send their children to the school in the midst of the controversy. She and teacher Barbara Henry form a powerful bond through the experience, and do not miss a day of school the entire academic year.

1961
As the school year ends, parents begin sending their children back to the school. By the beginning of the next school year, the elementary school is completely integrated.

In the aftermath of the crisis, Ruby's family suffers serious retribution: her father is fired from his job, her grandparents are asked to leave the tenant farm that they worked, and her beloved teacher Barbara Henry is not invited back the next year.

1964
Norman Rockwell paints *The Problem We All Live With*, a painting that will become famous for its depiction of Ruby entering the school with the federal marshals.

1995
The Story of Ruby Bridges, a children's book written by Robert Coles and illustrated by George Ford, is published.

1999
Bridges founds The Ruby Bridges Foundation, whose mission is "to change society through the education and inspiration of children."

GLIMPSES OF YOUTH

Ruby Bridges's mother allowed her six-year-old daughter to make the choice as to whether to confront the protesters at the William Frantz Elementary School, or to simply stay home that morning from school. Ruby, on her own, decided that she would go.

"Once they realize we are, indeed, their children, and we are, indeed, everywhere, every myth, every lie, every innuendo will be destroyed once and for all."

—HARVEY MILK
supervisor, 5th District, San Francisco

Harvey Milk became a leader simply by being the person that he was.

SEEKING JUSTICE

It was November 8th, 1977. The 5th District of the city of San Francisco had just elected Harvey Milk to its Board of Supervisors. Until then, the man had tried and failed three times to become an elected official. Supervisor Milk's political tenure would advance human rights in historic ways, and his name would echo through history less for what he did than for who he was. Harvey Milk was the first openly gay man ever to run for public office in the United States–and win.

HE STARTED A MOVEMENT BY SHINING A LIGHT IN THE DARKEST CORNERS

It is important in understanding the impact Harvey Milk had on the social landscape to reflect first on the political landscape of the United States in the 1970s. Liberal and conservative politicians across the country refused to be photographed with gay men like Milk because of the potentially explosive political consequences. The Supreme Court of the United States had, until then, regularly upheld laws that either limited or negated the rights of gay people, in one case supporting the rights of an employer to fire a man when his sexual preference became known.

Like millions of other gay people, Harvey Milk lived with the overwhelming pressure of having to hide the person that he was. He grew up a popular athlete, became a military man, an investment banker on Wall Street, and then a camera shop owner in San Francisco. There, he was a magnanimous populist, a gregarious neighbor, and a political activist. He was an energetic lover of life, with refined tastes that ran from opera to gourmet cuisine. Yet, despite his success, he never had a real place in society that he could openly call his own, until the day that he decided to fight back.

The core tenet of the philosophy Harvey Milk created in his life was that the best way for gay men and women to protest was to just be themselves with friends, family, and coworkers, and acknowledge openly who they were. This approach would become his way of life.

Supporters would carry Milk on their backs through the streets of the city after several of his groundbreaking political victories. "The establishment…white, very powerful, non-gay…had to deal with me," he would say. "Once they realize we are, indeed, their children, and we are, indeed, everywhere, every myth, every lie, every innuendo will be destroyed once and for all."

During his life, Harvey Milk recorded a tape to be played only in the event of his assassination. On that tape, he reflected on a life of commitment, passion, and foresight: "I stood for more than just a candidate…. [I stood] as part of a movement." He said about the people for whom he worked to bring justice: "There's hope for a better world…. There's hope for a better tomorrow. You can't live on hope alone, but without it, life's not worth living." He always abhorred the notion of secrecy and said, in a chilling moment, "If a bullet should enter my brain, let that bullet destroy every closet door."

An assassin ended Harvey Milk's life with two bullets to the head on November 27th, 1978. In life and in death, Milk changed the social landscape, opening hundreds of thousands of doors for people just like him around the world, people who had buried parts of themselves in secret closets. For millions of people around the world, he will live on in memory as the politician who made it all right for them to just be themselves.

1930
Harvey Bernard Milk
is born to Bill and Minerva
"Minnie" Milk in
Woodmere, New York.

1943-1944
Harvey is raised
in a supportive home with his
older brother, Robert.
Milk realizes that he is gay by the
time he is fourteen.

1944-1947
Harvey becomes
a popular high school student
and athlete, playing both
basketball and football. He learns
as a teenager to manage a double life,
keeping his homosexuality
a secret.

1947-1951
Milk attends the New York State
College for Teachers at Albany.

1951
After graduating from college,
Milk joins the Navy and reaches the
rank of chief petty officer, serving in
the Korean War. He is dishonorably
discharged when it is discovered
that he is homosexual.

1956
Milk becomes a teacher
of high school math and history in
Woodmere and moves in
with a gay man.

1972
Milk moves to San Francisco.
He founds the Castro Valley
Association, a grassroots organization
of local merchants, established to
lobby San Francisco City Hall
to give gay people and their
businesses more power in
what is a fiercely anti-homosexual
political climate. Milk becomes a
charismatic and much-loved activist
around the city.

1977
Harvey Milk becomes the first
openly gay person in U.S. history
to be elected to a significant public
position when he joins the Board of
Supervisors of San Francisco.

His charm, personality,
and political skills carry the day, so
that some of the most powerful politicians in San Francisco become
key allies. As a result of Milk's
efforts, Mayor George Moscone signs
the nation's first gay rights bill.

1978
Harvey Milk and Mayor Moscone
are assassinated on November 27th
in their offices at City Hall
by a disgruntled former member
of the Board of Supervisors.
Forty thousand mourners will
gather beneath the grand rotunda
of City Hall, where Milk
worked and died,
for a candlelight vigil.

1979
The year after the assassination,
one hundred thousand demonstrators
march on Washington, D.C.,
to demand that civil rights be
guaranteed to all gay people.
As they go, the marchers chant
"Harvey Milk lives."

GLIMPSES OF YOUTH

As a teenager, Harvey Milk used his
extra money to buy tickets to the
Metropolitan Opera.

"Where, after all, do universal human rights begin?
In small places, close to home—so close and so small that they cannot
be seen on any maps of the world."

—ELEANOR ROOSEVELT
social activist, writer, and speaker

Eleanor Roosevelt became a leader
listening to the needs and aspirations of the downtrodden

SEEKING JUSTICE

It was a radiant energy–a powerful and disciplined presence–that set Eleanor Roosevelt apart, and helped make her one of the most powerful advocates for social justice that the world had ever known. During her years as First Lady of the United States, from 1933 to 1945, she reshaped what had historically been a passive role. She provided a voice for the powerless, created the foundations for the passage of legislation that would end child labor and protect the rights of workers, and broke down barriers for women in sectors as diverse as radio broadcasting and politics. Meeting her, one would not have guessed that she grew up plagued by self-doubt.

SHE GAVE VOICE TO THE LEAST POWERFUL

She was shy and lonely as a child, longing for the consistent attention of an alcoholic father who drifted in and out of her life. She yearned for the acceptance of her mother, who rejected her early in life for having looks that she deemed too plain. Simply growing up became a painful journey of rejection and fear. "I was always afraid of something, of the dark, of displeasing people, of failure. Anything I accomplished had to be done across a barrier of fear." And still, in her lifetime, this woman would soar on the back of personal strength to erect a vision of social justice to change the world.

As First Lady of the United States, she represented the interests of the least powerful to her husband, Franklin Delano Roosevelt, the 32nd president of the United States. "I have access to the President," she would later explain. "And if I don't use that access to do things that need to be done for people, I would be sorely remiss and irresponsible." During the Great Depression, she made regular pilgrimages to the worst corners of poverty. "We do not dare to use even a little soap," said a father from Oregon, "when it will pay for an extra egg or a few more carrots for our children." "Can you be so kind," began another man in Pennsylvania in 1934, "as to advise me as to which would be the most humane way to dispose of myself and my family.... No home, no work, no money. We cannot go along this way." She had a rare ability to inspire in people a vision for a better life, no matter how bad it had become.

The experience of healing herself would be the foundation for much of what she accomplished in life. "One thing I believe profoundly: We make our own history," she would write. "The course of history is directed by the choices we make and our choices grow out of the ideas, the beliefs, the values, [and our] dreams." By confronting one fear at a time, she successfully challenged from the inside all the self-limiting preconceptions left by her childhood. "The encouraging thing," she would write, "is that every time you meet a situation, though you may think at the time it is an impossibility and you go through the tortures of the damned, once you have met it and lived through it you find that forever after you are freer than you ever were before." The heights she achieved in her career as a statesman, a speaker, a writer, a diplomat, and a visionary are testament to the transformation that ensued.

"People were absolutely drawn to Eleanor Roosevelt," Nina Gibson, her granddaughter, said of her. "Her presence was felt the moment she came into a room." Adlai Stevenson characterized her legacy this way: "What other human being has transformed the existence of so many? She walked into the slums and ghettos, not as a tour of inspection, but as one who could not feel contentment when others were hungry." As head of the United Nations Human Rights Commission, she would champion the Declaration of Human Rights manifesto that would be her crowning achievement. It codified her philosophy for a world community that was just beginning to understand the concepts she had spent a lifetime considering. "Where after all do human rights begin?" she wrote. "In small places, close to home–so close and so small that they cannot be seen on any map of the world. Yet they are the world of the individual person: the neighborhood he lives in; the school or college he attends; the factory, farm or office where he works. Such are the places where every man, woman, and child seeks equal justice, equal opportunity, equal dignity, without discrimination. Unless the rights have meaning there, they have little meaning anywhere."

1884
Eleanor Roosevelt is born to Elliot and Anna Hall Roosevelt in New York on October 11th, 1884. She is the niece of the 25th president of the United States, Theodore Roosevelt.

1887-1894
Eleanor grows up in a family of economic abundance and privilege, but one also characterized by emotional poverty. Her father, whom she reveres, struggles with alcoholism, and fails to create a consistent emotional connection to his family. Her mother is detached and judgmental. Eleanor develops a painful lack of self-confidence and a constant insecurity.

1899
When she is fifteen, Eleanor's parents send her to finishing school in Europe.

1905
At twenty, Eleanor marries Franklin Delano Roosevelt, a distant cousin. They have a natural rapport and a powerful relationship in emotional, intellectual, and political realms.

1905-1918
Eleanor bears six children within eleven years.

1918
At thirty-four, Eleanor discovers that her beloved husband has been having an affair with Lucy Mercer, a family confidante and Franklin's personal assistant. She braces for a long period of healing, and in the end chooses to stay with her husband, but to create a separate, independent identity.

1918-1921
Equipped with a new vitality and sense of self, Eleanor begins the passionate pursuit of a broad series of political causes close to her heart, including powerful economic and social reforms to abolish child labor and to establish the country's first minimum wage.

1921
Franklin develops polio and begins a seven-year battle.

1924-1935
At the request of friends and the family's doctors, Eleanor rekindles in her husband interests in the outside world, pulling him from his deeply personal physical struggle to the needs and concerns of a world outside. Several histories describe her as "his eyes and ears."

1945
After Franklin Roosevelt's death, President Harry Truman appoints Eleanor to be a delegate to the United Nations.

1962
Eleanor Roosevelt dies at the age of seventy-eight, after a scintillating life charged with action and duty for causes of social justice around the world that she has championed tirelessly. On her death, President John F. Kennedy calls her "one of the great ladies in the history of this country."

GLIMPSES OF YOUTH

Eleanor Roosevelt was terrified of speaking in public. As a teen, she often lost control of her voice. Nevertheless, she became one of the great leaders and speakers of her time, thanks to her ability to overcome difficult hurdles.

"The morning of November 14 federal marshals drove my mother and me the five blocks to William Frantz. In the car one of the men explained that when we arrived at the school two marshals would walk in front of us and two behind, so we'd be protected on both sides.... 'Ruby Nell,' she said as we pulled up to my new school, 'don't be afraid. There might be some people upset outside, but I'll be with you.' Sure enough, people shouted and shook their fist when we got out of the car, but to me it wasn't any noisier than Mardi Gras. I held my mother's hand and followed the marshals through the crowd, up the steps into the school. We spent that whole day sitting in the principal's office. Through the window, I saw white parents pointing at us and yelling, then rushing their children out of the school. In the uproar I never got to my classroom."

–RUBY BRIDGES HALL
The Education of Ruby Nell

"Swing low, sweet chariot. The song drifts gently into the night, as forty thousand stand beneath the grand rotunda of City Hall where Harvey Milk worked and died. At midnight, the crowd melts quietly away. Candles are left to shimmer on the bronze statue of Abraham Lincoln sitting in front of City Hall, the lights casting a multitude of tiny shadows. The mourners turn to walk back toward Castro Street, where it seems right for this night to end. After years of searching and drifting, Castro Street had become Harvey's hometown, and he had worked to make it a hometown for tens of thousands of homosexuals from around the world. The mayor of Castro Street, that was Harvey's unofficial title. And now the mayor of San Francisco and the mayor of Castro Street lie dead. What is left is the dream and its lengthening shadow."

–RANDY SHILTS
The Mayor of Castro Street: The Life and Times of Harvey Milk

SEEKING JUSTICE

"When Admiral Halsey said good-bye to [Eleanor], he told her it was impossible for him to express his appreciation for what she had done for his men .... 'She alone had accomplished more good than any other person, or any group of civilians, who had passed through my area. In the nine months left to me as COMSOPAC, nothing caused me to modify this opinion ....

When I say that she inspected those hospitals, I don't mean that she shook hands with the chief medical officer, glanced into a sun parlor, and left. I mean that she went into every ward, stopped at every bed, and spoke to every patient: What was his name? How did he feel? Was there anything he needed? Could she take a message home for him? I marveled at her hardihood, both physical and mental, she walked for miles, and she saw patients who were grievously and gruesomely wounded. But I marveled most at their expressions as she leaned over them. It was a sight I will never forget.'"

–ADMIRAL WILLIAM F. HALSEY
from *Eleanor and Franklin, The Story of Their Relationship,* by Joseph P. Lash

cour·age

1.
The state or quality of
mind or spirit that
enables one to face
danger or fear with
confidence and
resolution; bravery

in·teg·ri·ty

1.
Steadfast adherence
to a strict moral or
ethical code

2.
The state of being
unimpaired; soundness

3.
Honesty; freedom from
corrupting influence or
motive; uprightness

pres·ence

1.
A person's demeanor,
especially when it
commands respectful
attention

2.
A supernatural
influence felt to be
nearby

CHAPTER 9

A LEADER BECOMES A LEADER
BUILDING EMPIRES

"If you build it, [they] will come."

— line from the movie **Field of Dreams**

A LEADER BECOMES A LEADER
BUILDING EMPIRES

It is a famous story made into a famous movie. Ray Kinsella, a farmer in Iowa, rallies his friends and family to build a baseball field on his rural plot of land. He does not have enough money to pay his mortgage, and there are no baseball teams in sight that are in need of a field. But soon, on a foundation built of faith and human possibilities, a baseball stadium rises from the dirt that once hosted rows of corn, and a mysterious call goes out to legendary baseball players of every stripe and every era.

It is an emblematic story, one that rings true for every child who has ever built a sand castle at the ocean's edge to capture grand and imaginary places set against the endless promise of a summer's afternoon.

A leader who comes to build places of lasting value must first conceive of an irresistible vision, and then do what needs to be done to make that vision inevitable.

Walt Disney was a struggling animator who believed that children and adults alike would delight in a real place made from the stuff of storytelling, imagination, and wonder. In 1955, he opened the first Disneyland theme park in Anaheim, California. Ollie Johnston, one of Disney's early animators, described Disney's exceptional capacity to communicate a new vision: "I was just spellbound by [him]. Walt was a great actor. A wonderful, spontaneous actor. He'd be telling something and say, 'Like this,' and he'd get up and act it out and have you laughing at what he was talking about, and sure enough, you could visualize what he was presenting to you. It was amazing."

Bill Gates left a promising undergraduate career at Harvard, driven by an insistent vision that personal computers would someday dominate our personal and work lives as a vital new force of efficiency and creativity. As he left the university, he founded a company called Microsoft, and set out to create the operating system software for microcomputers. In the late 1970s, he led a mission that appeared irrational: "Our slogan from the very beginning was 'a computer on every desk in every home.'"

Katharine Graham lost a husband who was leading the family business, but quickly found inside a vision of herself as a woman who could build an international publishing conglomerate. She was shy and unsure of herself, and said of those early days: "Being a woman in control of a company–even a small company, as ours was then–was so singular and surprising in those days that I necessarily stood out.... The business world was essentially closed to women. At least through most of the 1960s, I basically lived in a man's world, hardly speaking to a woman all day except to the secretaries."

Graham was a fish out of water. But she was an innovator who acted before her time, building assets of sustaining value that went beyond the standard of the time. Her company's value would multiply fourteen times in one ten-year period under her leadership.

Such leaders travel out of time, into the dream of empire building, inventing the future out of today's line of software script, or from an artist's rendering, or from the plates of a printing press.

They honor their dreams when they put pen to paper and begin. They shape our future from a passion for what people can achieve. Suspending judgment, they create from the simple wonder of what is possible next.

"In the lexicon of youth, there is no such word as 'fail.'"

—WALT DISNEY
founder of the Walt Disney Company

Walt Disney became a leader in creativity
by engineering kingdoms dedicated to the happiness of children

BUILDING EMPIRES

It was July 25th, 1955.

Flames danced sporadically on the streets of Fantasyland from an undiscovered underground gas leak. The Mark Twain steamship sailed for the first time, but sank as it went down the Rivers of America from the weight of too many passengers.

The asphalt on Main Street got so hot that women's high-heeled shoes sunk deep into the newly laid cement. Managers ran armloads of cash from the ticket windows to the bank, just in time to make payroll. Visitors jumped fences, and some pretended to be friends of the celebrated founder just to get into this new place they called Disneyland.

HE BUILT AN EMPIRE FROM HIS IMAGINATION

It was the opening day in Anaheim, California. Walt Disney had launched his first theme park, an adventure in business innovation and a giant leap forward for a successful film and animation business that had enchanted viewers around the world with stories about a mouse named Mickey, and the classic animated film *Snow White and the Seven Dwarfs*.

In 1955, the original budget for the park was four and a half million dollars. It would eventually cost seventeen million dollars to complete. (Disney would have to sell his home in Palm Springs to finish paying for the project.) All in all, two million boxed feet of lumber, a million square feet of asphalt, five thousand cubic feet of concrete, and fifty thousand cubic feet of earth went into the massive building project. Only a third of the park was fully operational the day the company decided to launch.

Walt Disney's dream, a theme park that would unleash the unbridled imagination and joy of children around the world, would become the most visited tourist attraction in the United States, and the foundation of one of the most enduring entertainment brands in history.

He later would say of his grand adventure in Anaheim, "I could never convince the financiers that Disneyland was feasible, because dreams offer too little collateral."

But Walt Disney did not need collateral, because he was a visionary leader who understood the power of imagination and the power of ideas. Here was a person willing to chase a dream that had no precedent, that would never bear up under the pressures of corporate decision-making or market focus groups. Instead, the Walt Disney Company rose from the stuff of Mickey Mouse and Tomorrowland, and from a willingness to float a partly capsizing boat down a river on July 25th, 1955. The founder risked everything his successful company had created to transform a little-known town in California, so that visitors from around the world could come and let go of their cares.

Walt Disney grew up in a family that struggled to make ends meet. His father moved the Disneys many times when Walt was a boy, from job to job and town to town, working at various times as a carpenter, farmer, railroad machinist, postal carrier, and hotel manager. In the days of Walt's youth, a new urban economy was overtaking the rural landscape of Thomas Jefferson's pastoral America. Constantly on the move, Walt's parents never gave up on the idea that they could travel back to an earlier simplicity, to a place in their country's imagination that gave birth to a decent set of values, and a warm, family-centered way of life.

Neither did their son. Disneyland would bring the carpenter, the postman, the hotel manager, and explorer of Disney's midwestern childhood to life.

The founder, reflecting on the giant impact that Disneyland had on popular culture, explained the kind of energy he brought to his new visions: "In the lexicon of youth, there is no such word as 'fail.' Certainly we have all had this confidence at one time in our lives, though most lose it as we grow older. Perhaps, because of my work, I've been lucky enough to retain a shred of this youthful quality."

"From the very beginning–and much to our surprise–Microsoft was pretty successful. In large part, that was because we lived and breathed software, stopping only to eat and catch a few hours of sleep here and there. We were totally hard-core about succeeding right out of the gate."

–BILL GATES
founder, Microsoft Corporation

Bill Gates became a leader in software, building on the power of very small things.

BUILDING EMPIRES

He dropped out of Harvard in 1975 at the age of nineteen, believing passionately that personal computers would change the way people work, and that he could ride the waves of the coming sea changes in industry to great success. He started a company called Microsoft with a partner, Paul Allen, and together they wrote streams of code in rudimentary languages such as Basic, Fortran, and Cobol. He would create one of the most dominant corporate forces in the history of capitalism–and none of it would have happened without his now-mythic preparation habits and one critical meeting in a corporate conference room.

HE BUILT AN EMPIRE ON TINY LITTLE BITS

The meeting in that room took place on a fall day in 1980 at an IBM office in Boca Raton, Florida. At the table for Microsoft was its exhausted founder, Bill Gates, and two senior executives. The small start-up company's young leader had been up several nights in a row crafting his sales presentation, an example of the intense style of preparation that would become his personal trademark. It had been just four years since the young renegade had set in motion his impossible mission of creating the operating software standard for the new personal computing industry. Annual sales were just seven million dollars at the time.

For IBM–Big Blue, as it is called–there were eight sharply focused executives and two attorneys at the table. The Microsoft executives led a company of fewer than forty people in Seattle, Washington. Their IBM counterparts were part of a thirty-five-billion-dollar business whose workforce numbered half the population of the state in which Microsoft resided.

Gates dazzled his audience that day with the most detailed product specifications, designed in advance to meet the complex needs of IBM's soon-to-be-introduced personal computers. He charmed them with a crystal vision of where the market for personal computers was heading. He left no questions unanswered, traversing virgin technical territory with steady, unbending confidence and focus. He was so powerful in his presentation that day that an IBM decision maker later explained that it was Gates's incredible mastery of his discipline and product that won him and his colleagues over.

At that meeting, the eight IBM executives agreed in principle to give Microsoft ownership of the operating system that would be the heart and soul of nearly every personal computer that it, and many other companies, would manufacture for the foreseeable future. The IBM executives had come that day to pick a supplier for an operating system. They left the meeting with the skeleton of an understanding that would put Microsoft on an unprecedented course to greatness.

To understand the magnitude of that meeting, consider this. By 1992, just twelve years later, Microsoft's operating system would be installed on seventy-five percent of the world's personal computers. Today, Microsoft is one of the wealthiest companies on the planet, with an eighty-six percent market share and thirty-six billion dollars in sales. It is the most profitable business in existence, and has a near-monopoly on information systems, guiding the flow of computing information around the world.

And it all started at a meeting in Boca Raton that was attended by just thirteen people. Bill Gates built an empire on the power of bits–tiny pieces of information–that together form software, the nexus of power in the new information age. But he first built his empire on meticulous preparation–arriving at a meeting as head of a small start-up company, and leaving it with the fundamental assets necessary to become a world power in information systems for many years to come.

"To love what you do and feel that it matters–
how could anything be more fun?"

–KATHARINE GRAHAM
owner, The Washington Post Company

Katharine Graham became a leader in journalism
building on the power of truth, one story at a time

BUILDING EMPIRES

"When I look back over my long life, if there is one thing that leaps out at me it is the role of luck and chance in our lives. From [a] particular string of accidental happenings, all the rest followed." It is an unexpected and powerful statement from one of the most influential business women of the twentieth century. At the time she wrote it, Katharine Graham, the principal owner of The Washington Post Company, was one of publishing's great entrepreneurs. According to longtime *Post* editor Ben Bradlee, she was a woman who "set a course [for the paper] and took it to the very top ranks of American journalism in principle and fairness."

SHE BUILT AN EMPIRE ONE STORY AT A TIME

Katharine Graham was born in 1917 to a prosperous family, and grew up in rarefied surroundings. Her father, Ernest Meyer, was a successful innovator on Wall Street whose personal fortune soared to astonishing levels early in his life. He was the first president of the World Bank, and served as an early governor of the United States Federal Reserve.

While Katharine's family's economic circumstances were healthy, her emotional roots were anything but. She wonders openly in her autobiography, *Personal History*, whether her mother actually had the capacity to love her own children. Graham concluded that she, nonetheless, felt closer to her mother than to her father, who was, in her words, "a very distant and rather difficult figure." "Mother set impossibly high standards for us," she wrote. "She "creat[ed] tremendous pressures and undermin[ed] our ability to accomplish whatever modest aims we may have set for ourselves. Fundamentally, I think we all felt we somehow hadn't lived up to what she expected or wanted of us, and the insecurities and lack of self-confidence she bred were long-lasting."

As a teenager, Katharine dreamed of being a fashion model; although she enjoyed talk of the family business, she had no ambition to take it over. Her husband, Phil, served ably as the company's CEO, while she willingly played a background role, raising their children and managing the family affairs. However, after her husband's unexpected suicide at forty-seven, she was suddenly and unexpectedly thrust into the spotlight. She was so distraught by his sudden passing that her daughter, Lally, had to draft her comments to the board of directors, announcing that the family would not sell The Washington Post Company.

Katharine took over the role of CEO in 1963, when accidental happenings kicked into high gear. She writes in her book: "Throughout the first weeks, I felt I was wandering around in a fog, trying to grasp the rudiments: who did what, when, why, where, and how. It's hard to describe how abysmally ignorant I was. I knew neither the substance of the business and journalistic worlds in which I was moving nor the processes through which these worlds operated."

She would build a business that the world-renowned investor Warren Buffett said multiplied fourteen times in value in the short decade after his original investment in 1973. Yet her life story, the Pulitzer Prize-winning autobiography *Personal History*, explains that she came by her leadership position and eventual greatness as a kind of accidental tourist–moving through the events of her life, one surprise at a time, without a compass or a plan.

But what an accidental tourist this steady woman was. While her legendary father struggled for two decades to make the *Post* profitable, she absorbed the wisdom of confidants like Buffett, and built one of the great print and broadcast enterprises of her day. Ben Bradlee said that she possessed "the heart of a journalist" and "the head of a businesswoman," which made Katharine Graham "one of the greatest publishers of the last two centuries."

"I have always considered the daily paper a miracle of sorts," she explained at the end of her life. A miracle made possible by a leader who took the reins in a time of ultimate duress and set the business on a course for gravity and greatness, breaking critical stories across four decades.

1917
Katharine Meyer is born to Agnes and Ernest Meyer, June 16th, 1917. Her parents become powerful international figures in business, finance, and high society. Their appetites for hard work and socializing make them a distant influence as she and her sister grow up.

1933
When Kay is just sixteen, her father purchases The Washington Post Company out of bankruptcy for eight hundred twenty-five thousand dollars.

1934
Meyer gets her first exposure to the newsroom, working for the *Post* as a copy editor.

1939
After a stint as a reporter at the *San Francisco News*, Meyer joins *The Washington Post* full time in the editorial department.

Meyer meets Phil Graham, and falls hopelessly in love. The handsome, erudite man would be warmly welcomed into the family publishing business as associate publisher after the two get married.

1963
After an illustrious career building the newspaper, Phil Graham loses his battle with manic depression and alcoholism, and takes his own life. Katharine Graham becomes president of The Washington Post Company. Hers becomes a struggle to find sufficient inner fortitude to succeed as a woman in a realm that, up until then, had been dominated by men.

1971
Despite enormous business pressures, Katharine Graham decides to publish the Pentagon Papers. These top-secret documents provide important insight into the machinations of the Vietnam War.

1972
The *Post* begins its historic coverage of a burglary at the Democratic National Committee headquarters at the Watergate office building in Washington, D.C.

1974-2000
Graham's power and influence grows internationally as she builds a highly successful multimillion dollar communications empire. She works and socializes in circles that include individuals who have been witnesses to the birth of the modern world.

2001
Graham dies from injuries suffered in a fall on an icy sidewalk at age eighty-four. Arthur Sulzberger, chairman emeritus of The New York Times Company, captures the impact she has had: "She will be remembered as a truly remarkable woman.... She used her intelligence, her courage, and her wit to transform the landscape of American journalism."

Katharine Graham's father was Jewish by faith; her mother was Lutheran. She experienced early on some of the insidious effects of anti-Semitism, as she was barred from joining certain groups or living in certain areas of Washington, D.C.

"His first studio was in a corner of a garage.
His gleaming newest cost two million dollars, covers several hundred thousand square feet, is...as immaculate as a hospital, and as functional as a research scientist's dream laboratory. Five years ago the little band of Disney faithful totaled two hundred souls; today the payroll shows eleven hundred. Until three years ago the studio had never made a long picture; today's schedule calls for three 'features' and twenty-six 'shorts' a year. That promises the final production of a serpent of celluloid nineteen hundred miles long, of which each linear foot will consist of sixteen 'frames,' or individual pictures.... *Pinocchio*, for instance, required over half a million final drawings. And before each final single–or multiple–color drawing is ready for the camera it has been preceded by an incalculable number of preliminary sketches, moulding the characters, the situation, the action, the expression, to their final needle-focus of perfection. Walt'll be thirty-nine this winter."

–ERIC LOREN SMOODIN
Disney Discourse: Producing the Magic Kingdom

"He had spent a sleepless night on Delta's red-eye flight from
Seattle to Miami, memorizing business and technical information for his meeting with IBM. He, Steve Ballmer, and Bob O'Rear were scheduled to meet with IBM executives at their Entry Level Systems facility in Boca Raton. Gates carried with him the final report on how the jeans-and-tennis-shoe programmers at Microsoft could work with the white-shirt-and-wingtip crowd at IBM on Project Chess, codename for the top secret IBM effort to develop a personal computer....

On the nonstop, overnight flight to Miami, the three friends, wired from excitement and lack of sleep, pored over the final report, making last-minute revisions and corrections.... The report proposed that Microsoft supply four high-level languages–Basic, Fortran, Cobol, and Pascal–for IBM's new microcomputer. More significantly, it proposed that Microsoft develop the computer's disk operating system, DOS."

–JAMES WALLACE
Hard Drive: Bill Gates and the Making of the Microsoft Empire

BUILDING EMPIRES

"Then came...the years of learning, of stumbling, of fun,
of some achievement, progress, mixed with big smelly eggs on the floor–laid and cleaned up or just shoved under the rug until the stain soaked through. The fascinating thing–and the thing to remember– is that if you have enough going for you in the way of momentum and luck, everyone looks at the developing pattern of the rug, whether it's an Oriental design or the stain from the egg, and says, 'What a beautiful rug.' And pretty soon we're telling ourselves, 'It's a hell of a rug we've made.'"

–KATHARINE GRAHAM
Personal History

i·mag·i·na·tion

1.
Using the creative
power of the mind;
resourcefulness

2.
The power of the mind
to form images,
especially
of what is not present
to the senses

prep·a·ra·tion

1.
The state of having
been made ready
beforehand; readiness

2.
That which makes
ready, prepares the
way, or introduces; a
preparatory act or
measure

3.
Activity leading to
skilled behavior

grace

1.
Seemingly effortless
beauty or charm of
movement, form, or
proportion

2.
Elegance and beauty
of movement or
expression

CHAPTER 10

A LEADER BECOMES A LEADER
THROUGH INNOVATION
AND CREATIVITY

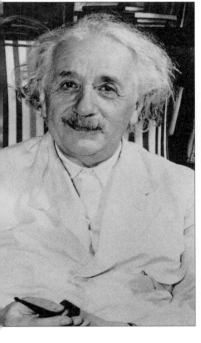

"Making the simple complicated is commonplace;
making the complicated simple,
awesomely simple, that's creativity."

—CHARLES MINGUS
virtuoso bassist, band leader, and composer

A LEADER BECOMES A LEADER
THROUGH INNOVATION
AND CREATIVITY

A popular filmmaker of considerable renown described his creative process for *Time* magazine: "Art is…being available to accidents that fall into your lap. The ideal way to work on a [film] is to ask a question you don't know the answer to."

Michelangelo di Buonarroti was an artist from the Italian Renaissance whom many consider to be the greatest sculptor and painter who ever lived. He spent a lifetime asking questions to which he had no answers. Michelangelo was an adventurer in truth, working to uncover rich realities from human history's most important dramas. He was an adventurer in beauty, who opened the world's eyes to the potent power of creativity in his masterwork, the Sistine Chapel ceiling. He chose profound questions to pursue, and rendered in his art essential stories that captured basic human challenges: David taking on the giant Goliath, the Madonna mourning her son who has just died. In marble or paint, he illuminated for audiences noble aspects of humanity from the physical attitudes of his subjects–a stealthy warrior preparing himself to beat an invulnerable giant, or a mother holding the body of a fallen child. How, he wondered, did David fell the mighty Goliath? During three years of study and incessant carving, Michelangelo injected his sculpture, *David*, with a radiance that takes a pilgrim's breath away.

In his seminal biography of Michelangelo, *The Agony and The Ecstasy*, Irving Stone described how Michelangelo found the power to create the *David* from his evolving relationship with a block of marble: "He had lived with this block for several months now, studied it in every light, from every angle, in every degree of heat and cold. He had slowly come to understand its nature, not by cutting into it with a chisel but by force of perception, until he believed he knew every layer, every crystal, and precisely how the marble could be persuaded to yield the forms he needed." Michelangelo spent more time getting to know the block of stone he would carve than he did sketching likenesses of what he wanted the *David* to be.

MIT researchers have postulated that the process of creativity and innovation is, in fact, one of discovery. A successful innovator attunes himself to a question–to a block of stone–and uncovers what is unseen, the hidden truth that lies under the surface.

An innovator's life begins when the process of discovery begins. Marie Curie had a mysterious and demanding connection to an element that had not yet been detected. She would spend a half a lifetime in her laboratory discovering an element she called radium. Louis Armstrong's embrace of a brass trumpet saved him from the streets of New Orleans, and allowed a street urchin to take flight above the poverty that held him down. Albert Einstein's fascination with the potentials of subatomic particles helped him open passageways to mysteries of the universe that continue to unfold in the most advanced physics laboratories around the world.

There is an intimate connection between a leader who creates, and the physical world in which he finds himself. "It sure was the greatest thing that ever happened to me," Armstrong would say of the first time he picked up a trumpet at a youth detention center where he was incarcerated at age twelve. "Me and music got married at the home." In some ways, the instrument he discovered saved his life. It gave him a way off the streets, a channel for a deep and insistent genius, and a means of expression that allowed an impish, passionate young boy to travel music's international corridors, where he would lead a revolution in expression, language, and sound.

A leader's journey is both solitary and public. It arises from an inner knowing that enables the leader to travel light, irrespective of the context–whether exploding freely in the bustling village square, or sequestered alone in the silence of a laboratory.

"Because [Michelangelo] would take no time off for friends or rest or social life," Irving Stone explained, "[his friend] Balducci accused him of trying to escape the world by fleeing into marble. [Michelangelo] admitted to his friend that he was half right: the sculptor carries into the marble the vision of a more luminous world than the one that surrounds him. But the artist was not in flight: he was in pursuit. He was trying with all his might to overtake a vision."

> "Life is not easy for any of us, but what of that?
> We must have perseverance and above all confidence in ourselves.
> We must believe that we are gifted in something, and that this thing,
> at whatever cost, must be attained."

—MARIE CURIE
pioneer in the field of radiology

Marie Curie became a leader,
achieving scientific advances with passion and focus.

INNOVATION AND CREATIVITY

She was a gritty woman. You can see it in the photographs of her in the laboratory. She stands immersed in the solitude of discovery, up to her elbows in pitchblende residue (uranium ore), an elusive fragment of pure radium hiding under the surface of tons and tons of radium residue. She would spend three years digging it out.

THE PASSIONATE FOCUS OF MARIE CURIE

The precision it took, the dogged determination, and what seemed to many the foolish commitment to an improbable result, carried her forward–morning to night, day to weekend, for months on end. She would not stop working until one-fiftieth of a teaspoon of pure radium was available for all the world to study and understand. "Sometimes I had to spend a whole day stirring a boiling mass with a heavy iron rod nearly as big as myself," she recalled. "I would be broken with fatigue at day's end." Cornell University professor Ernest Merritt put the vast undertaking in perspective: "The task undertaken by Madame Curie in attempting to separate [the unknown substance] from pitchblende was somewhat similar to that of a detective who starts out to find a suspected criminal in a crowded street…. The problem was one of extreme difficulty; but it had all the fascination of a journey into an unexplored land."

Her willingness to soldier on–to reach that elusive goal with unbounded focus–made the study of radioactivity possible. Such was the life and work of Marie Curie.

Her intensity was forged in occupied Poland, where she was born in 1867. Her father was a professor who believed that the only way to fight an oppressive foreign occupier was to become educated, and to educate others. Some of her ancestors were forced to go on death marches, yet her family carried on, risking prison to help the impoverished learn to read and write. They set their course on an intellectual revolution, believing that as long as the candle of fierce scientific imagination burned true, no one could end the progress of a society. As a young woman, Marie taught illiterate women to read and write. Her father would lose his job when the authorities found him passing on knowledge illegally.

As a young girl, her life was riddled with loss. Her mother fought tuberculosis for much of her life, and avoided physical contact with her children. Marie lost her mother emotionally first, and then physically; the disease killed her when Marie was just twelve years old. That loss, the death of her sister when she was eight, and her father's extraordinary dedication to political resistance shaped her fundamentally. She would suffer all of her life from an acute depression that was a stubborn remnant of her early childhood losses. At the end of her life, the only time she could remember delighting in the world was when, at age fifteen, her parents sent her away to the country to recuperate with her uncle's family after an emotional collapse brought on by the tremendous pressures at home. But she stayed gritty, and found an extraordinary love in the form of a intellectual companion in science, and romantic companion in life–Pierre Curie. She stayed gritty, and tracked down that one-fiftieth of a teaspoon of pure radium to win the Nobel Prize. She stayed gritty, and rose from poverty to live the second half of her life in comfort. She would rise from these circumstances on a new faith–that science could deliver restoration and new life to sick people everywhere.

It is something of a miracle that she survived the circumstances of her upbringing, but when she did, she found herself removed from pain and loss. A million people were helped in World War I by her efforts to deliver X-ray technology to wounded troops across Europe. Since then, the science of radioactivity has delivered healing to untold millions of sick people around the world. "I am among those who think that science has great beauty," she explained. "A scientist in his laboratory is not only a technician, he is also a child placed before natural phenomena, which impress him like a fairy tale…. If I see anything vital around me, it is precisely that spirit of adventure, which seems indestructible."

MARIE'S LIFE

1867
Marie Sklodowska is born in Warsaw, Poland, to parents who are both teachers. They will imbue in her a love of learning.

1879
As a young girl growing up in a totalitarian society, Marie joins a student revolutionary organization, demonstrating the kind of courage and capacity for brazen innovation that will characterize her adult life.

1887-1897
She dreams of studying at the Sorbonne, in Paris. Her family has little money, and her attendance will depend on her willingness to save for years.

1891
At twenty-four, Marie arrives at the Sorbonne to study. She majors in mathematics and physics, and her remarkable ability to focus and learn drives her toward an exceptionally successful career as a scientist.

1895
Marie marries her beloved fiancé, Pierre Curie, another driven discoverer. His hope is to "spend life side by side" with her "in the sway of our dreams."

1900
Marie Curie first describes the property of radioactivity–that radiation is released as an element's nucleus naturally breaks down (not the result of a chemical reaction). She will spend a considerable part of her career promoting the use of radium to diminish human suffering.

1898-1902
The Curies work together–shoulder to shoulder–in a small, leaking shed. After an intensive period processing chemicals in spartan conditions, they isolate the element's radium, and are awarded the Nobel Prize in 1903 for their discovery of radioactive elements.

1904
Pierre dies in a freak accident when he is hit by a horse-drawn cart.

1911
Marie Curie wins a second Nobel Prize in chemistry for her work determining the atomic weight of radium.

1914
Marie Curie becomes the head of the Paris Institute of Radium and cofounds the Curie Institute.

1934
She dies from overexposure to radiation, as her exuberance for her search and the lack of understanding of the dangers of working with radiation take a fatal toll. Her groundbreaking work set the stage for dramatic advances in nuclear medicine, and prepared the way for one of the most important advances in twentieth-century science, as the world discovers the structure of the atom.

GLIMPSES OF YOUTH

At an early age, Marie Curie lost an older sister to typhus and her mother to tuberculosis. She grieved for them, but with help from her father, became a star student in school, and spent her free time dreaming of becoming one of the first women research scientists in the world.

"Imagination is more important than knowledge. Knowledge is limited. Imagination encircles the world."

—ALBERT EINSTEIN
visionary physicist

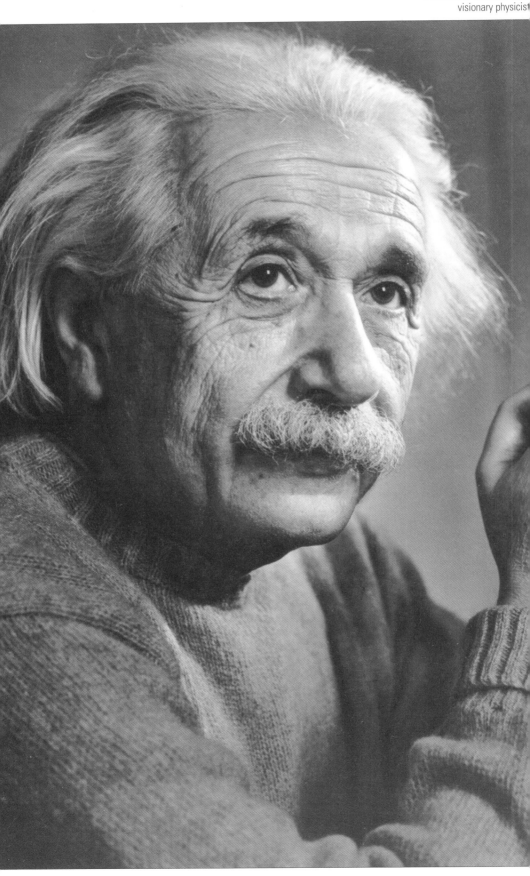

Albert Einstein became a leade
marrying imagination, smarts, and intuition to change the worl

INNOVATION AND CREATIVITY

He didn't speak until he was three years old. Early in his schooling, he regularly had failing grades. As a young man, he often forgot his own address because he was so enamored of a thought drifting through his head. But this visionary physicist named Albert Einstein could think things that had never existed before, and his willingness to imagine beyond the bounds of what was accepted would change the way people saw themselves and the world forever. Einstein had a way with thoughts akin to the way that some of the literary giants–William Shakespeare and John Donne–had with words.

HE COMBINED SCIENCE WITH IMAGINATION TO CHANGE THE WAY WE SEE THE WORLD

There is a famous story about how difficult it is to understand Einstein's cornerstone theory of relativity. Arthur Edington, a celebrated astrophysicist of the day, was asked, "Is it true that only three people on earth understand Einstein's theory of relativity?" He replied with a famously wry wit: "I am trying to think who the third person is." To explain it to regular folks, Einstein provided a wonderfully simple image: "When a man sits with a pretty girl for an hour, it seems like a minute. But sit on a hot stove for a minute, and it's longer than any hour. That's relativity."

Simple enough. Now, just overlay that metaphor onto the laws of physics and the space-time continuum, and you've pretty much got a complete handle on it.

Einstein was an enigma from the beginning. Caring little for the things of this world (he had a famously meager salary), he cared a great deal about the implications the new technologies had for the security of the planet. By nature, he was a pacifist, yet he donated a handwritten copy of his famous theory of relativity for auction to help finance the Allied war effort during World War II, because of his natural enmity for tyranny. (His manuscript sold for six million dollars.) He was a loner whose life of the mind kept him enchanted for hours at a time, but whose overwhelming charisma and success brought him as much attention as a modern-day rock star. People forget that reporters and photographers regularly followed him around in a day when *People* magazine was nowhere to be found.

Some historians believe that he was expelled from school at age fifteen because his ideas were so profound that they were confusing the academic process. (You get the sense reading his biography that many of his teachers simply did not understand what he was talking about.) His mind was so fertile, so on fire with the unlikely combination of rationality, instinct, and imagination that constitutes genius, that the institutions around him could not comprehend or contain what he was. "It is nothing short of a miracle," he said, "that modern methods of instruction have not yet entirely strangled the holy curiosity of inquiry." One teacher tellingly commented that "your mere presence here undermines the class's respect for me."

As a young man of just twenty-five, he was often spotted pushing his young son in a stroller around Bern, Switzerland, as he filled a notebook with symbols and ideas. Just a year later, the contents of that overflowing notebook would undergird Einstein's first published theories of physics, which would forever change the scientific community's understanding of the material world. The unassuming young man with the wild and wavy hair made a series of scientific statements in his mid-twenties that jolted the world with the truths they told about how the universe really works.

Einstein's science was one part art and one part philosophy, expressing in essential truths a deep satisfaction with the way the world manifested itself. He understood the power of passion and imagination–for him, they drove all greatness, and linked humanity to the mysteries and creativity that bring the things that are truly valuable. "I am enough of an artist to draw freely upon my imagination," he told the *Saturday Evening Post*. "Imagination is more important than knowledge. Knowledge is limited. Imagination encircles the world."

ALBERT'S LIFE

1879
Albert Einstein is born in Ulm, Germany, to Pauline and Hermann Einstein. Neither parent is particularly adept in science and math. In grammar school, their son is such a poor student that they believe he has a learning disability.

1885-1894
Albert develops an extraordinary ability to learn complex disciplines on his own, and becomes an exceptional student of advanced math and science.

1900
Einstein graduates from the Swiss Polytechnic School in Zurich with a degree in physics.

1894-1905
The young man creates theories of physics that so confound the academic community that he finds himself isolated from the mainstream thinkers of his time.

1905
Einstein works as a patent examiner in Bern, Switzerland. People around town observe him scribbling notes on a pad of paper that he keeps inside his son's baby stroller. These inspirations become the fundamentals of the theory of relativity that he creates in his spare time.

1905-1915
Einstein's theory of relativity vaults the young genius to the forefront of modern science, and shakes the foundation of humankind's very perception of the universe.

1916
Albert demonstrates that light has mass, that it bends, and that space and time are actually one continuum. He shatters vast systems of established science, suggesting that there is a sensible order to the universe.

1921
Einstein receives the Nobel Prize at the age of forty-two.

1933
Terrified by the vicious politics of hatred, Einstein fears for his family's safety and flees Europe for the United States.

1935
Einstein joins the faculty of Princeton University as the head of the mathematics department. He famously asks for "a desk, some pads and a pencil, and a large wastebasket–to hold all of my mistakes." He will spend his time at Princeton inventing quantum physics.

1955
Albert Einstein dies in his sleep, leaving the world to ponder his profound scientific breakthroughs. He inspires a vast audience with simple, powerful insights into our very existence: "One cannot help but be in awe [when one] contemplates the mysteries of eternity, of life, of the marvelous structures of reality."

GLIMPSES OF YOUTH

Albert Einstein didn't speak until he was three, was an indifferent student early on, and was even expelled from school by one headmaster. As an adult, nothing kept him from thinking thoughts that would shake the roots of physics and humanity's worldview.

"My whole life, my whole soul, my whole spirit is to blow that horn."

–LOUIS ARMSTRONG
jazz innovator and international humanist

Louis Armstrong became a leade
transmitting his joy for music across all boundarie

They called him "Pops." They called him "Satchmo." From all walks of life and every tier of a fractured society, they came to hear him play his trumpet, because the jazz music that he played was so rich, so dynamic, and so utterly new. In the early years of the twentieth century, it seemed to deliver to those who listened a new sense of freedom, just as the modern systems and cities were simultaneously imposing new kinds of constraints. He would spend his life inventing a singular trumpet sound, which soared and ripped and tore and swung and exploded from him in high-pitched reels of exuberant, compassionate, and vivid celebration. He would record some of the era's most transcendent sides, from his "Cornet Chop Suey" masterpiece to what many called a life-changing recording of "West End Blues." In Louis Armstrong, the music seemed to emanate from a place of such singular joy that it would rain down on people who came near, like sheets of spray off a pounding August waterfall.

HIS JOY PENETRATED THE MOST RESISTANT BARRIERS

Red Stewart, a jazz contemporary of Armstrong's and an unabashed fan, described the effect his hero had on him, and on the city of Chicago, when he first landed there in 1922: "I went mad with the rest of the town. I tried to walk like him, talk like him, eat like him, sleep like him. I even bought a pair of big policeman shoes like he used to wear and stood outside his apartment waiting for him to come out so I could look at him."

Armstrong made it his mission in life to transmit the revolutionary sounds of the new music to what he perceived to be a broken world. And the man certainly knew what a broken world looked like. His childhood was set on the ashes of desperation, in one of the toughest neighborhoods in New Orleans. Armstrong's beginnings had little to do with the magnetism Stewart describes, or with the delight the jazz master would come to deliver to audiences around the world. In fact, Armstrong spent the better part of his early life in a monumental struggle just to find his way off the streets of New Orleans. His father abandoned the family at an early age. His mother was likely a prostitute, turning tricks in a neighborhood called Storyville, a dilapidated, crime-ridden island of urban despair. The prostitutes, drug dealers, and street musicians who lived in the neighborhood became young Louis's surrogate family, and kept order, disorder, and time on the side streets of a city bursting to the rhythms of the new music called jazz. Armstrong wandered into the Big Easy at the turn of the twentieth century without a father, without a compass, and without a nickel in his pocket. "You must realize, it was very shaky during my days growing up in New Orleans," he would later write. "You had to fight and do a lot of ungodly things to keep from being trampled on."

A collision with the law would have the young boy committed to a youth detention center for one and a half years. It would, ironically, be in detention that he would receive his first real taste of family, team play, and formal training on the trumpet. He would pick up the trumpet, and ride it on a journey to the heart of a new American art form. He would tour racially intolerant landscapes to become an international symbol of everything jazz. But one of his signature achievements was something very personal. He left all that glittered on the world's stages to journey back to the stability, decency, and sense of family that he first experienced at the Colored Waif's Home where he had been sent as a child. He would, over a long stretch of time, find out for himself what it really meant to have a home, and what it really meant to be part of a family.

His wife, Lucille, described what it was like for her forty-two-year-old husband to experience his own Christmas tree for the first time: "I gave him his Christmas present ... and Louis was still laying up in bed watching the tree, his eyes just like a baby's eyes. 'No, don't turn them out. I have to just keep looking at it. You know, that's the first tree I ever had.'"

Modern-day trumpet giant Wynton Marsalis, reflecting on Louis Armstrong's achievement, said, "Louis Armstrong's overwhelming message is one of love. When you hear his music, it's of joy.... He was just not going to be defeated by the forces of life. And those forces visit all of us."

"Marie Curie left behind no written testament revealing how well she felt she had lived up to her youthful aspiration of developing herself and contributing to the welfare of others. But there was no doubt about her accomplishments in the minds of two of the major physicists of the 20th century, Ernest Rutherford and Albert Einstein. Both of these distinguished friends and colleagues published a eulogy on the occasion of Marie Curie's death.... [Rutherford] wrote: 'The many friends of Madam Curie around the world, who admired her not only for her scientific talents but also for her fine character and personality, lament the untimely removal of one who had made such great contributions to knowledge, and, through her discoveries, to the welfare of mankind.' For his part, Einstein in 1935 published *Marie Curie in Memoriam*. He praised her for acting on the conviction that she was always 'a servant of society.' He attributed her discovery of radium and polonium 'not merely to bold intuition but to a devotion and tenacity in execution under the most extreme hardships imaginable.'"

—NAOMI E. PASACHOFF
Marie Curie and the Science of Radioactivity

"If most of [Einstein's] articles were short, there was not one among them that did not contain marvelous new ideas destined to revolutionize science, or acute and profound remarks penetrating to the most obscure recesses of the problem under consideration and opening in a few words almost unlimited perspectives. The work of Einstein is above all a 'work of quality' in which elaboration and detailed development are not to be found. His articles might be compared to blazing rockets which in the dark of the night suddenly cast a brief but powerful illumination over an immense unknown region.... Einstein always was able—and this is the mark of his genius—to master all the questions which faced him and to envisage them in some novel aspect which had escaped his precursors.... Example after example could be cited: each would prove to us the originality and genius of a mind which can perceive in a single glance, through the complex maze of difficult questions, the new and simple idea which enabled him to elicit their true significance and suddenly to bring clarity and light where darkness had reigned."

—P.A. SCHILPP
Albert Einstein: Philosopher-Scientist

INNOVATION AND CREATIVITY

"From listening to his records, I already had some inkling of the warmth and power of the man, but I was totally unprepared for that remarkable penetrating awareness underneath the genial, easygoing manner. All his senses seem to receive impressions of you; you feel he's not so much sizing you up as opening his mind to you, like a receiver set. You can't fake it with Louis. He can tell."

—MAX KAMINSKY
Jazz: A History of America's Music, by Geoffrey C. Ward and Ken Burns

fo·cus

1.
A center of interest or activity

2.
Close or narrow attention; concentration

gen·ius

1.
A strong natural talent, aptitude, or inclination

2.
Distinguished mental superiority; uncommon intellectual power; superior power of invention or origination of any kind

joy

1.
To fill with ecstatic happiness, pleasure, or satisfaction

2.
Exhilaration of spirits; intense delight

CHAPTER 11

A LEADER BECOMES A LEADER
WITH ATHLETIC
PROWESS

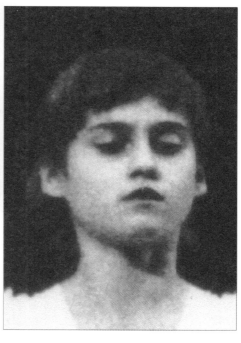

"The most important thing in the Olympic Games is not to win but to take part, just as the most important thing in life is not the triumph but the struggle. The essential thing is not to have conquered but to have fought well."

–PIERRE DE COUBERTIN
author of the Olympic Creed

A LEADER BECOMES A LEADER
WITH ATHLETIC
PROWESS

His is a now famous sports story. His father gave him his first golf club when he was just three years old. By the time he was eight, he had won his first junior world championship. By the time he was fifteen, he had become the youngest player in history to win the U. S. Junior Amateur championship.

Tiger Woods would go on to create a staggering record of performance, one that many believe will make him the greatest golfer in history. But what gets lost in the stories of his glowing achievements are the years of disciplined, deliberate practice as he worked through the specific physical challenges of a complex sport.

Woods began with the same passion for golf that the young Wolfgang Amadeus Mozart had for the piano. What set Woods apart from other young golfers blessed with talent and vigor was an insistent and long-term desire to learn, to analyze his game, to overcome limitations, and to change and improve his strokes over many years of diligent and focused practice.

Sport is about movement. Athletes combine a series of complex, learned movements to achieve a certain competitive goal. Tiger Woods lifts his left heel before swinging down on the ball. Nadia Comaneci cartwheels to a stand. Michael Jordan works on the trajectory of his jump shot. All are practiced elements that help make up a broad arsenal of tools; when combined with focus and passion, these tools make athletes forces to be reckoned with.

But physicality is not the exclusive domain of athletes. Pat Metheny, the renowned jazz guitarist, is famous for returning to his hotel room after a gig to work through the finer motions of his craft that escaped him that evening. He refines imperfect musical moments to capture riffs that become crucial elements of his future harmonic arsenal. Successful athletes share with Metheny an ability to grow in self-awareness–to study and understand their own body's progress–and to find specific ways to improve. Renowned sports instructor and tennis expert Vic Braden encourages his disciples to review video of their matches, and to experience their own performances from the outside to make important strides forward.

Dan Goodgame explained in *Time* magazine the exceptional drive for improvement that makes Tiger Woods such an important athlete: "Consider…what Woods did right after he dominated the 1997 Masters. He studied videotapes of his performance: blasting 300-yard drives, hitting crisp iron shots right at the pins, draining putts from everywhere. And he thought, as he later told friends, 'My swing really [needs work].'"

Butch Harmon, Tiger's coach early in his career, went on to explain: "When Tiger turned pro, he was long but wild. So he worked on that and has led in total driving. He had trouble controlling his distance with the irons, so he worked on that, and now leads in greens in regulation…. He was always a good putter, but he's worked to be more consistent. Whatever he sees as a weakness in his game, he turns into a strength." It is the essence of dedication, the willingness to work over long periods of time on the specifics of a craft, that makes leaders leaders, and that makes athletes able to compete at every level of competition.

Tiger Woods explained his experience pursuing the standards he set for himself: "People thought it was asinine for me to change my swing after I won the Masters by 12 shots…. 'Why would you want to change that?' Well, I thought I could become better."

Nadia Comaneci described her own approach to building her competitive advantage: "After a while, if you work on a certain move consistently, then it doesn't seem so risky. The idea is that the move stays dangerous and it looks dangerous to my opponents–but it isn't to me. That is my secret."

Michael Jordan's athleticism is unparalleled in the eyes of most observers, but his approach of consistently working through the fundamental mechanics of basketball resonates for all leaders seeking to reach new heights in their chosen field: "When you understand the building blocks, you begin to see how the whole operation works. And that allows you to operate more intelligently, whether it's in school, business, or … raising a family," he says. "You have to monitor your fundamentals constantly… [and] the fundamentals never change."

"Winning is not always the barometer of getting better."

–TIGER WOODS
world champion golfer

Tiger Woods became a leade
using a different method for measuring success

WITH ATHLETIC PROWESS

He was the winningest freshman in the history of the sport.

It was 1997. Tiger Woods was in his first year as a professional golfer on the Professional Golfers Association Tour. The twenty-two-year-old newcomer from Stanford qualified for fifteen of the PGA golf tournaments that year, stunning the golf world by winning four of them. He qualified to play in the Masters, one of professional golf's preeminent tournaments, and broke a four-day scoring record that had stood for thirty-two years. By the end of the year, Woods would accrue tournament winnings and endorsements that topped a staggering sixty million dollars.

HE REDEFINED SUCCESS ONE STROKE AT A TIME

And yet, having reached the top echelon of his professional sport in his first year out, Tiger Woods decided to recreate his golf swing.

To reinvent your swing as a professional golfer is to reinvent the very foundation of your game. It is something like an academic recreating the core tenets of a lifetime's philosophy, or a musician composing on piano rather than guitar after decades of success.

It was a strategy fraught with risk, one that had proven disastrous for a litany of celebrated professional players who had come before and failed. Tinkering with your swing as a professional golfer, history taught, would often relegate the best of champions to the middle of the pack.

And yet, he reinvented.

He hit balls, viewed tape, and then hit more balls. He realized that a looser grip and tighter hip turn would slow his swing sufficiently to give him better control of his clubhead as he whipped down on the ball with ferocious velocity. He could maintain championship performance, he believed, while he altered his swing in ways that would give him a greater variety of options on the course, and that would make the energy in his swing work better for him. He took his game apart, one element at a time, and slowly, over many months, put it back together—one hip rotation, one grip, one physical motion at a time.

His performance changed markedly. He played mediocre golf at first. The press and players collectively whispered that it had just been freshman luck his first year, that he would never again dominate the sport as he had in 1997. But he weathered the downturn, and as 1998 progressed, his game started coming back together at a level no one could have anticipated. And one day, like a sea captain who had disappeared across a distant watery horizon, Tiger Woods was back.

Tiger Woods had always been on an odyssey to uncover the magnificence of his competitive spirit ever since he first played as a little boy. His process of reinvention and self-education was one that he had employed at several significant turning points. These were the paces he put himself through to become a champion. This was the skill-building process that made the sport exhilarating and the point of view that set him apart from the rest of the pack.

In 1999, he won eight PGA Tour titles and eleven events overall. Between 2000 and 2001, Tiger won four consecutive Grand Slam titles, an accomplishment that came to be known as the "Tiger Slam."

Throughout his career, he has kept front and center the core philosophy that had carried him through the period of loss, reconstruction, and gain:

"Winning is not always the barometer of getting better."

"Always improve your game

—MICHAEL JORDAN
professional basketball playe

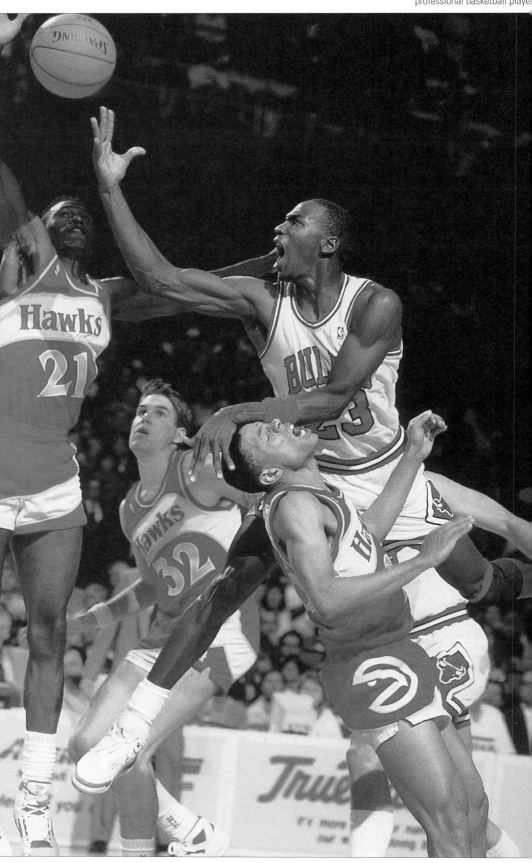

Michael Jordan became a leade
improving his craft and his game every single day

WITH ATHLETIC PROWESS

It was early on the morning of March 13th, 1984. It was the day after the North Carolina Tar Heels unexpectedly lost the Eastern semifinal NCAA tournament game to the Indiana Hoosiers. Tar Heel players were cleaning out their lockers *en masse*, packing sports equipment into bags, and making postseason plans as they tried hard to take their minds off the stunning disappointment from the night before. Only one of the Tar Heel players was somewhere else that morning. Michael Jordan spent those early morning hours in the team gymnasium, practicing the jump shot that had failed him too many times the night before.

HE MADE PRACTICE HIS BUSINESS

That was the work ethic of Michael Jeffrey Jordan. Michael Jordan realized early on in life, as he struggled to beat his older brother, Larry, in one-on-one basketball, that his greatest adversary in becoming a championship player would be his own physical limitations. And so, when he joined the NBA in 1984, although gifted with an ability to jump like few others and with rare speed to match, Jordan knew that to become a champion in the National Basketball Association he would have to reach new levels of skill, mastery, and perseverance. He knew that the road to the world championship was crowded with standout players and powerful teams who never quite got to the finish line.

The early buzz on Michael Jordan as he was coming out of college was very positive. It was clear that he was a player of unusual potential. He rose through the ranks of Dean Smith's famously hierarchical system at North Carolina faster than any college freshman before him. But seven years and seven seasons into his NBA career, Jordan and his Chicago Bulls had yet to win the NBA title. It was particularly frustrating for Jordan, who was now regarded as the best player in the league. He had entered the league with a mediocre jump shot and had risen to become one of the most effective shooters the league had known. He was always the first to arrive at practice and the last to leave. In pick-up games, he would work on weaknesses and the smallest vulnerabilities in his game, while most players showcased their flashiest stuff. James Worthy, prominent forward for the Los Angeles Lakers, said of him in David Halberstam's seminal biography, *Playing for Keeps*: "It is rare that a naturally gifted player would have such intense practice habits."

But it wasn't enough. Jordan worked smart, innovating where others were standing still. He hired his own personal trainer, to help him meld his explosive bursts of energy and speed with grinding power wrought from sheer physical strength. He created an early-morning "breakfast club" with Scottie Pippen to improve their roundball rapport every day before the Bulls' regular practice. And then, on June 1st, 1991, seven years into the league, thousands of practice sessions and adjustments to his game later, the Bulls at last won the NBA world championship. Michael Jordan was so overcome by his team's victory over the Lakers that he sat in the locker room after the game, hugging the championship trophy and weeping.

We all know how the story ends. Michael Jordan went on to become the greatest basketball player ever to lace up a pair of sneakers, and the Bulls went on to win five more world championships under his leadership. His joy for the game and passion to succeed were unparalleled and unforgettable, lifting the Bulls to incredible heights and fueling passion around the world for the sport of basketball. There is a little-known story about his father James's concern for a hard-working, underpaid assistant coach at North Carolina from Michael's college days. Roy Williams worked hard to push Michael's game forward on the court, and equally hard off the court to pay his own bills. James Jordan had such admiration for the man's work ethic that he made the coach a wood stove by hand to help him reduce his heating costs. Michael Jordan would go on to make basketball history, with his own Jordan-made wood stove set firmly in his heart, creating a fire for victory that still blazes in the imaginations of basketball fans any time they hear the sound of nothing but net.

"I loved being in the air and how it feels, how it feels on your body.

—NADIA COMANECI
recipient of first perfect '10' in Olympic history

Nadia Comaneci became a leader in gymnastics
raising the bar in the Olympics to find greatness

WITH ATHLETIC PROWESS

The Olympics had been in turmoil for four years.

From terrorists capturing and then assassinating eleven Olympic athletes in the Olympic Village in Munich, West Germany, in 1972, to twenty-five countries boycotting the summer games in Montreal, Canada, in 1976, politics, sometimes violent, had shaken the very roots of the Olympic movement.

SHE RAISED THE BAR AND TASTED PERFECTION

But even after the horrifying occupation of the Olympic Village in 1972, the summer Games went on four years later in Montreal. There, in the midst of roiling controversy over countries politicizing the event for nationalistic purposes, a solitary, diminutive fourteen-year-old gymnast from Romania succeeded in floating above it all. Her performance had no equal before, and has not been equalled since. She riveted the world, refocusing its attention from the noise of politics to the fundamentals of physical prowess and beauty in motion that seemed to transport her audience every time she performed.

Nadia Comaneci was just four feet, eleven inches tall when her presence enchanted the world. Her teammates, standing on the opposite side of the balance beam from where she would mount, would have just been able to make out her head rising above the four-foot apparatus. The eighty-six-pound athlete back-flipped, twisted, and leaped her way through a series of exercises that made many professional observers wonder if a gymnast had somehow learned to fly. It was as if the dark intensity in that young woman's gaze had propelled her up, higher, higher, until her lithe, picturesque form broke free from all natural limitations to find a new plane on which to perform.

She had it all that summer in Montreal: unequalled balance, exceptional strength, physical stamina, steady composure, uncommon presence, and an ability to explode in midair that astonished everyone who saw the young Romanian perform. When the perfect score for her exercise on the uneven bars–the first "10" in modern Olympics gymnastics history, dating back to 1896–hit the scoreboard, it appeared simply as "1.0," because no one had rigged the digital display to go up to "10." The Olympic administrators and technicians had not anticipated that it would ever be necessary.

The crowd roared its approval for the sheer magnificence of her history-making performance, while Comaneci and her Romanian coach, Bela Karolyi, recoiled in stunned silence, believing that "1.0" might have reflected some enormous penalty from the judges for an error that no one had detected during the performance. When she realized that "1.0" meant "10," Nadia Comaneci emerged from the shadows of intense personal discipline and athletic desire to acknowledge and embrace the international community's overwhelming appreciation. "One of my teammates said, 'I think it's a 10, but they don't know how to make a 10…so I went up on the floor and waved.'"

Only Nadia Comaneci knew how to make a "10" that night. She raised the bar for gymnastic performance to the top rung. Her very presence in Montreal that year quieted the political instability and confusion, and shifted the focus to the simple truths and triumphs that make the Olympics what they are. Her transcendent success was unexpected for a fourteen-year-old, who later confessed to a reporter that all she had hoped for that night was that her "mum" be watching her performance on television. That, as she set a new Olympic standard in gymnastics and soared above the Olympics to new, uncharted territory.

"Nobody in golf works harder than Tiger Woods.
The Saturday night before the final round at the PGA,
he was the last player on the range and putting green. He didn't want
to leave until it was right. And while 18-under-par was enough for
Tiger to take [Bob] May into a playoff and survive,
it still wasn't up to his standards."

–TIM ROSAFORTE
Raising the Bar: The Championship Years of Tiger Woods

"Even in pickup games,
he had become unusually purposeful. There was a tendency
in games like this, when there were no coaches around, for players to
resort to what they did best, to reinforce their strengths and to avoid going
to any part of their game that was essentially weak. But Jordan … was constantly working on the weaker part of his game, trying to bring it up.
It was … one more sign of his desire to be the best."

–DAVID HALBERSTAM
Playing for Keeps: Michael Jordan and the World He Made

WITH ATHLETIC PROWESS

"The whole crowd exploded
and I was jumping up and down like a crazy rooster.
There are moments you never forget.
Even though time goes by and certain events fade out,
this is one of the moments I'll never forget."

–BELA KAROLYI
U.S. women's Olympic team coach
from "Nadia Comaneci Remembers Perfect 10," by Nancy Amour, Associated Press

ed·u·ca·tion

1.
A program of
instruction of a specified
kind or level

2.
The knowledge or skill
obtained or developed
by a learning process

3.
An instructive or
enlightening experience

work eth·ic

1.
A set of values based on
the moral virtues of
hard work and dili-
gence

2.
A set of principles of
right conduct

stan·dard

1.
An acknowledged
measure of comparison
for quantitative or
qualitative value;
a criterion

2.
Established or widely
recognized as a model
of authority or
excellence

CHAPTER 12

A LEADER BECOMES A LEADER
MANIFESTING BEAUTY

"All a musician can do is to get closer to the sources of nature, and so feel that he is in communion with the natural laws."

–JOHN COLTRANE
jazz innovator

MANIFESTING
BEAUTY

From pain to joy, from darkness to light. In their work, they made of sadness, beauty; of loss, hope; and of failure, reconciliation and resolution. The late creative genius Ray Charles said of inspiration, "Every music has its own soul; be true to the soul of the music." The artists portrayed here were true to the soul of their work.

Ansel Adams, Georgia O'Keeffe, and Martha Graham all honored in their art the best of the human spirit. They transformed places of quiet desperation into unexpected places of new life revealed. In art, they delivered the glory of the human experience. Mixing compassion, pity, courage, hope, creativity, passion, and sacrifice, they produced tantalizing visions of a world transformed from the stuff of their studios: a sudden flow of oils to a canvas, the flowing body of a dancer, a glass negative emerging from a basin of shadowy chemicals in a photographer's darkroom. All three journeyed to a wilderness that no one had ever seen. All three brought to their international audiences revelations that, ever since, have led to new understanding and awakened spirits.

Georgia O'Keeffe painted canvases on an easel she set up outside her home in New Mexico, in the backseat of a broken-down Model A. The open-air studio she created in that car seemed to craft a bridge between the metallic world of New York City, where she had recently been living, and the flowering desert, where she had taken refuge. The car's rear window opened on breathtaking vistas of the natural world of the Southwest. O'Keeffe conducted startling images of enormous flowers and sky-framed animal bones into the paintings developing before her. It was as if the energy of the natural world around that car moved through the steely frame of yesterday's Model A, and joined with O'Keeffe's white-hot imagination to create works that would sanctify her audiences by presenting an utterly new expression of nature.

Ansel Adams hauled his cumbersome camera, tripod, and camping equipment up the sheer mountain faces of Yosemite in northern California. He knew there were deep truths available for the world to experience in the mist of an early spring dawn that only he could capture. Those solitary settings were his workshop. Stunning photographs of virgin territory emerged from his imagination with a disquieting intimacy. His images of a towering and majestic nature made audiences pause, and sometimes gasp.

Martha Graham brought to her dance a fiery honesty and passion for movement that would transfix audiences for generations. Broad gestures of falling, thrusting dancers débuted in Graham's choreography, and showed the way to a new dawn in the world of dance. Her father, a doctor whose stern gaze could sometimes terrify his daughter, drove her forward with a singular admonition early in life: "Martha, you must never lie to me, because movement never lies, and when I see your body I'll know you're lying." Rage, love, passion, and a fluid emotional nakedness would come to define her revolutionary work, and help create a new field of abstract dance, a discipline that had previously been defined by controlled and studied movement. She would tell her truths in bold triumphs such as *Appalachian Spring* and *Letters to the World*. Her unexpected images and fevered expression would attract future innovators, such as Merce Cunningham, Paul Taylor, and Twyla Tharp, to her company. "Our arms start from the back because they were once wings," she would explain, and then she would go off to find new expressions in the bodies of dancers who would follow her vision, and for audiences that would absorb her bold new approach.

O'Keeffe, Adams, and Graham lived like phantom angels, reinvigorating society by prying loose pieces of the night sky to let light shine through. In their work, they illumined the dark corners of clouded perception that sometimes become our homes. No one who experienced the energy could return to their former selves without at least first wondering what else might be possible.

T. S. Eliot wrote of the power of the artist's process in his seminal poem *The Four Quartets*:

> We shall not cease from exploration
> And in the end all our exploring
> Will be to arrive where we started
> And know the place for the first time.

Country music legend Dolly Parton explained how she understands the role of leadership: "If your actions [create] a legacy that inspires others to dream more, learn more, do more and become more, then you are a...leader."

Artists lead through their ceaseless exploration. Like the first spring cardinal in the backyard of a Kentucky morning–there on the backyard fence, illumined by the sun, and resonating with new life–the artist inspires us to become more than we already are.

THE ARTISTRY OF
ANSEL ADAMS 1902-1984

"There is a deeper thing to express–the return of humanity to some
sort of balanced awareness of the natural things–some rocks and sky.
We need a little earth to stand on and feel run through our fingers.
Perhaps photography can do this–I am going to try anyhow.'

–ANSEL ADAMS
nature photographer

Ansel Adams became a leader in photography,
stalking the beauty of nature with a knapsack and camera

MANIFESTING BEAUTY

Some have a passion for their life's work that approaches spiritual quest. They come to it as a kind of calling, and follow their paths with a verve and intensity that approaches the religious. That was the way of Ansel Adams.

HE STALKED THE BEAUTY OF NATURE

He began his artistic quest as a talented pianist, but he would leave this first love. It would be his passion for photographing the Sierras and Yosemite that finally won out. You get the feeling from reading his autobiography that the wisdom of the ages had called to him from those mountainous tracts, wound up stranded in a box, and only he had the key. The pull was that strong.

Ansel Adams would take the art of photography to a new level, so much so that the art form's patriarch and creative revolutionary, Alfred Stieglitz, would come to say of one of Adams's early portfolios, "These are some of the finest photographs I have ever seen."

His approach to art was grounded in purity and simplicity. The strenuous climbs he took to the heights of Yosemite to get his pictures, the explosive revelations from his experiences in nature, and the words he used to capture it all reveal the essential truths of art at a higher level.

For seventy years, he witnessed the changing mysteries of nature's landscape with an unequalled receptivity. He was a pioneer of the American West, hiking into the mountains alone with tripod, camera and supplies–waiting, watching.

But for all the stillness around him, he was in a constant race against time: to lasso the light of a white rising moon before it disappeared; to spray the nascent rays of dawn across his plate, as they illuminated ripe green pastures where bison had recently been grazing.

His genius lay in his attention to the finest details of the craft. He tracked seasons and weather patterns for months at a time, waiting for the right time to photograph a particular vista. He would produce hundreds of prints of the same photograph, spending days on end in his darkroom until he captured the spirit of the natural world in a fully realized image.

"There is still something incomprehensible to me about the photographic process," he would explain. "The physics of the situation are fearfully complex, but the miracle of the image is a triumph of the imagination. The most miraculous ritual of all is the combination of machine, mind, and spirit that brings forth images of great power and beauty."

It is hard to imagine such a passionate and singular vision. His words are our best window on the man:

"I was climbing the long ridge west of Mount Clark. It was one of those mornings where the sunlight is burnished with a keen wind and long feathers of cloud move in a lofty sky. The silver light turned every blade of grass and every particle of sand into a luminous metallic splendor; there was nothing, however small, that did not clash in the bright wind, that did not send arrows of light through the glassy air. I was suddenly arrested in the long crunching path up the ridge by an exceedingly pointed awareness of the *light*. The moment I paused, the full impact of the mood was upon me; I saw more clearly than I have ever seen before or since the minute detail of the grasses…the small flotsam of the forest, the motion of the high clouds streaming above the peaks…. I dreamed that for a moment time stood quietly, and the vision became but the shadow of an infinitely greater world–and I had within the grasp of consciousness a transcendental experience."

1902
Ansel Adams is born to Charles and Olive Adams in San Francisco, California. A year later, his parents move the family to a house with a beautiful view of the Golden Gate Bridge, setting the stage for the young boy to develop a lifelong passion for striking moments of natural beauty.

1905-1915
Adams is a child of extreme energy. He has such a difficult time focusing that his father decides to homeschool his only son. In an extraordinary display of support for the young boy's energy, Charles encourages him to spend as much time on the California dunes as he does learning to read.

1914
At twelve years old, Ansel gets inspired when he hears a neighbor play the piano. He asks his mother to bring home some piano books; according to his father, Ansel seems to learn to sight-read and play the instrument in a few short months.

1916
At fourteen, his parents give Ansel his first camera–a Kodak No. 1 Box Brownie. He encourages them to vacation in the mountainous region of Yosemite, a trip that will be the first of four consecutive annual sojourns, and the beginning of a lifelong love affair with the region.

1922
At twenty, Adams writes home to his beloved father, Charles: "Dear Father: I am more than ever convinced that the only possible way to interpret the scenes hereabout is through an impressionistic vision. A cold material representation gives one no conception whatever of the great size and distances of these mountains. Ansel."

1930
Adams decides that photography is his life's passion, and makes treks to the High Sierras and the Southwest.

1965
Adams's passion for photographing nature is matched only by his love of the environment. He spends a good part of his career advancing environmental causes, serving on the board of the Sierra Club for some thirty-five years and meeting with politicians, such as President Lyndon Johnson, to lobby for environmental policy.

1980
Adams is awarded the Medal of Freedom for his artistic achievements.

1984
On April 24th, Ansel Adams dies at the age of eighty-two. His genius for capturing nature's majesty in photographs has made him his generation's most exhibited photographer. In response to his passing, the United States Congress names two hundred thousand acres near Yosemite the Ansel Adams Wilderness Area.

Ansel Adams called his early years "the father to the man I became." He spent those years surrounded by nature, and often used his early memories as inspiration for the moods and visions that he captured later in his photography.

"Still–in a way–nobody sees a flower–really–
it is so small–we haven't time–and to see takes time,
like to have a friend takes time."

–GEORGIA O'KEEFFE
artist, painter

Georgia O'Keeffe was a leader and groundbreaking artist
making her subject the natural world of the Southwestern United States

MANIFESTING BEAUTY

Georgia O'Keeffe knew at a very young age what she wanted to do with her life. "I am going to be an artist," she told a twelve-year-old friend. "It [is] definitely settled in my mind." Growing up in a traditional farm family in Sun Prairie, Wisconsin, was difficult for a young girl bursting with energy, imagination, and unusual ambition. She recalled feeling like an outsider in the family. Her parents looked on her creative ways, she said, as if they were just "more of Georgie's crazy notions. They never approved of me.... My mother and I never agreed. I got so I would just not talk about the things I knew we would disagree about. I was going to be an artist."

SHE WAS A WITNESS TO WONDER

Her teachers recognized her prodigious artistic skills early on, and channeled them into the norms and styles of the day–"imitative realism," as it was called then. But her vision of the world and how to paint it had little to do with what she was taught in school. She got frustrated, left her studies, and soon found herself again on the outside of the cultural norms. "I was taught to paint like other people. I hadn't been taught a way of my own."

Until she met a teacher named Alon Bement in 1912. "His idea was to fill a space in a beautiful way, which was a new idea for me," she said years later, still shaken by the intrinsic wonder of that new idea. Sometimes in life, new ideas have a way of shaking your foundation and setting you free. Accepting Bement's concept of filling spaces in beautiful ways as a platform for a new beginning, she discovered that her voice and vision had at last found a natural home where they could exist comfortably. "I have things in my head that are not like what anyone has taught me," she explained to an interviewer. "Shapes and ideas so near to me…so natural to my way of being and thinking that it hasn't occurred to me to put them down."

Her challenge was not in finding her vision, as many artists struggle to do. Her challenge was in recognizing that her vision had a place in the world, and then letting it live powerfully, separately, and as an organic presence–with integrity, and as an end in itself.

Her life seems to have begun in the presence of a vivid, vibrating energy that enveloped, transfixed, and transformed her in an experience of dynamic dimension and primitive warmth. "My first memory is of the brightness of light," she recounts, "light all around…. I was sitting among pillows on a quilt on the ground…very large, white pillows."

It would be in this relationship, which she found transcendent, that she would come to live her days, and then to make an art that would help redefine American art. Her paintings would stop time with images of gigantic, bursting flowers and white animal bones strewn across a New Mexico sky. It was art as no one had seen it before–spontaneous and beautiful. As a human being, she was "absolutely living every pulse beat," said Alfred Stieglitz, one of the earliest pioneers of photography as an art form, and her eventual husband. "[Her works] were the purest, finest, sincerest things that had entered [the studio] in a long time."

She had an uncanny ability to capture the wonder and awe of the natural world around her. Where some would see sex in her welcoming blossoms, she told an observer that she simply saw life. Where others saw death in her images of bones, she said that all she saw was sky. "When I found the beautiful white bones in the desert, I picked them up and took them home, too. I have used these things to say what is to me the wideness and wonder of the world as I live in it."

Although she spent some prolific years in New York City, it was the great American Southwest that beckoned to her like those pillows full of light. When asked why she moved to such an isolated place as New Mexico to do her work, she laughed her womanly laugh, and responded simply that she did so because she could: "I'll paint what I see–what the flower is to me," she said of her most famous images. "But I'll paint it big, and they will be surprised into taking time to look at it–I will make even busy New Yorkers take time to see what I see of flowers."

GEORGIA'S LIFE

1887
Georgia is born in Sun Prairie, Wisconsin, to Ida and Francis O'Keeffe. She will be one of six children. As a young girl, she realizes that she wants to be an artist.

1890-1902
Growing up, Georgia begins to have visions of light imagery that dazzle her. As she starts to reveal a rich imaginative life to those around her, she realizes that her traditional farm family, although focused on education and independent thinking, considers "Georgie's notions" a distraction.

1905
At eighteen years old, O'Keeffe begins her college studies at the Art Institute of Chicago. Her relationship with formal training is strained, as her vision and the approach taught by the academic community of the time do not mesh. She falls into and out of art classes, and continues to seek external expression throughout her early adulthood.

1915
At twenty-eight, after a long hiatus from painting, O'Keeffe meets Arthur Dow, an expert in Asian art. Dow inspires in her the power and awareness to find her own voice.

1916
A friend of O'Keeffe shows some of her work to Alfred Stieglitz, the pre-eminent innovator in the photographic arts. He is so moved by what Georgia has accomplished that he immediately moves to showcase her art at his influential New York City art space, 291 Gallery. Stieglitz and O'Keeffe fall in love, and she becomes a favorite subject for him in his photographs.

1924
Alfred Stieglitz and Georgia O'Keeffe marry. The two will awaken in each other startling inspirations for art and discovery; theirs becomes one of the great relationships in twentieth-century art. Stieglitz describes her artistic approach as one of putting "a woman on paper."

1929
O'Keeffe vacations with a friend in Taos, New Mexico, and finds her new subject in the big sky vistas and sun-scorched expanses of the Southwest.

1946
Her husband and greatest admirer dies. O'Keeffe leaves New York to take up permanent residence in New Mexico. She unleashes a masterful series of landscapes, marrying the vibrant natural sensuality of her early work with the themes of mortality and the past.

1970
The Whitney Museum of American Art features an extensive retrospective of O'Keeffe's work that establishes her as one of the great forces in twentieth-century art. O'Keeffe releases an illustrated autobiography, *Georgia O'Keeffe*, which becomes a bestseller.

1986
Georgia O'Keeffe dies at the age of ninety-eight in Santa Fe, New Mexico. In her lifetime, she has created a new American art–explosive, sensual, open, and liberating.

GLIMPSES OF YOUTH

Georgia's parents were dairy farmers in Sun Prairie, Wisconsin. She received art lessons on the farm growing up.

"You are unique, and if that is not fulfilled, then something has been lost."

—MARTHA GRAHAM
dance innovator

Martha Graham became a leader in art and physical movement choreographing dance in ways that no one had experienced

MANIFESTING BEAUTY

She had a revelation in her late teens that she would become one of the great dancers of her time. After seeing the ballerina Ruth St. Denis perform, she enrolled in an arts college, and then auditioned for St. Denis's renowned Denishawn Company in 1916. The artistic director dismissed her out of hand, believing the young woman was too old, at the age of twenty, and too heavy to be a great dancer.

Undaunted, Martha Graham began a life's quest to create a new approach to dance, one that would help redefine the discipline. The very troupe that had rejected her soon offered her a spot because of her relentless focus and energy. She would find within the Denishawn Company a new approach to beauty that would emanate from a heart on fire.

SHE MADE DANCE A REFLECTION OF HER INNER LIFE

One of her students eloquently described the power of her presence and vision: "Everybody was hypnotized, absolutely magnetized by Martha. She opened our eyes to the arts. I was on fire." Her father, a doctor, was the first to impress upon her the meaning of the body's movements, and their importance in translating what is true. "Martha, you must never lie to me," he said, "because movement never lies, and when I see your body, I'll know you're lying." On the surface, it was a scolding, but underneath, it was an invitation to the elements within her that were already moving to places of vivid new expression, and that would one day rip open the curtains of the theater to reframe the very essence of dance.

Her rise from rejected novitiate to prominent artist was not an easy one. While her triumphs would one day be compared to the triumphs of Picasso in painting, she left the Denishawn Company in 1923 at age twenty-nine to pursue her own work–with no following, and no money in her pocket. Her dancers would take day jobs to pay the rent. "We didn't expect to be paid," one explained. "We almost didn't want to be, because, you know, it was complete dedication, like a sisterhood."

The commitment and passion felt by that sisterhood seamlessly transferred to the Martha Graham Dance Company when it débuted in 1927. The first audiences were enthralled with the works of this new rebel choreographer on the scene. Until that point, dance as an art form had been studied and rigid. Graham's work was an explosion of edges, a vital thrust of human emotion that embraced rage, passion, love, despair, desire, and desperation. Dancers dove, pelvises contracted, and floor work dominated her scenes. "I wanted to begin not with characters or ideas, but with movements," she said. "I did not want it to be beautiful or fluid. I wanted it to be fraught with inner meaning, with excitement and surge."

Graham's was an art of the natural. The power of what she achieved depended on finding dancers who could surrender themselves to movements that erupted from the depths of their very being. What was startling was how immediate the work was. When she first danced professionally, she told a reporter from the *Santa Barbara News*, "I could not do anything that I could not feel. A dance must dominate me completely, until I lose sense of everything else."

A fearless energy would unleash a remarkable body of work over a career that spanned six decades. As a choreographer, she explored Greek myths and retold core human dramas. "If it could be said in words, it would be," she said, "but outside of words, outside of painting, outside of sculpture, inside the body is an interior landscape which is revealed in movement." When she launched her majestic signature piece, *Primitive Mysteries*, in 1931, the *New York Herald Tribune* explained its power: It is "the most significant choreography which has yet to come out of America…. It achieves a mood which actually lifts both spectators and dancers in the rarified heights of spiritual ecstasy." *The New York Times* would capture the magnificence of what she had achieved in her career with this great compliment: "She had, in William Faulkner's apt phrase, put a scratch on the face of eternity." Dance was not something that Martha Graham did; it was what Martha Graham was. "I did not choose to be a dancer," she said. "I was chosen."

MARTHA'S LIFE

1894
Martha Graham is born in Allegheny, Pennsylvania, to Jane and George Graham. Her father is a medical doctor whose mission is to understand the source of human disease by analyzing a patient's physical movements.

1901-1916
Martha is a proficient athlete as a young girl. At the age of twenty-two, late for a dancer, she joins the Denishawn dance school, and falls in love with dance.

1926
After eight years with the Denishawn troupe, Graham launches her own company in a small dance studio at Carnegie Hall in New York City. Her vision is to "chart the graph of the heart" through her art. She believes that the body can express its inner turmoil, passion, and emotion. She unleashes a torrent of new movement in her work.

1927
Graham officially inaugurates the Martha Graham School of Contemporary Dance.

1938
Eleanor Roosevelt invites Graham to perform at the White House, where she performs a new work, *American Document*. She will perform for seven other American presidents.

1940-1955
Graham's career flourishes as she propels her art forward through stunning works such as *Appalachian Spring*, a collaboration with Aaron Copeland, and *Seraphic Dialogues*, a dance epic that tells the story of Joan of Arc.

1976
President Gerald R. Ford awards Graham the country's highest civilian honor, the Presidential Medal of Freedom. He calls her "a national treasure," and shines international light on the new genre of dance that she has helped conceive.

1991
Martha Graham dies of cardiac arrest.

In her career, she has collaborated with some of the finest contributors to modern culture, and created a new language for movement and expression that creates an important alternative to the classic school of ballet. She is remembered as a revolutionary in the arts of the twentieth century.

1998
Time magazine honors the legacy of Martha Graham, naming her Dancer of the Century.

2007
Eighty-one years after its inception, the Martha Graham Dance Company remains "the most celebrated dance company in the world."

GLIMPSES OF YOUTH

At seventeen, Martha Graham attends her first dance performance in Los Angeles. "That night, my fate was sealed," she explained. The experience changes her profoundly, and she enrolls in a junior college that focuses on the arts and begins her life's work.

"It was like a ballet, watching him in the darkroom jumping around and dodging and burning and saying, 'I want the sky to be richer,' and he really worked them over, and often it would take him a whole day before he got one print from a negative right. Once he did that he could make more prints but it was real, real labor. I don't know, half or forty percent of the creative process occurred in the darkroom."

—WILLIAM TURNAGE
Wilderness Society president and friend of Ansel Adams

"Georgia O'Keeffe is much more extraordinary than even I had believed—In fact I don't believe there has ever been anything like her—Mind and feeling very clear—spontaneous—and uncannily beautiful—absolutely living every pulse beat."

—ALFRED STIEGLITZ
photographer

MANIFESTING BEAUTY

"At my very first class, she took a piece of chiffon and held it over her head and walked with it in this pattern she uses on the stage. She wanted to show us how dramatic just a plain walk could be.

Now, I wasn't the first one who saw this. The girl I came to class with turned to me and whispered, 'Did you see that?' It was as if all the lights went out in the studio and a special spot came on. Her skin color changed as though she were in a spotlight. All of a sudden, there was this energy, and she flushed. I've seen her do it many times since. She could control it, like blushing. It was spooky."

—BERTRAM ROSS
student of Martha Graham
from *Martha Graham: A Dancer's Life*, by Russell Freedman

art·ist·ry

1.
The superior ability
that is attained by study
and practice and
observation

won·der

1.
One that arouses awe,
astonishment, surprise,
or admiration; a marvel

2.
An event inexplicable
by the laws of nature

3.
The presentation to the
sight or mind of
something new, unusu-
al, strange, great,
or not well understood

innovation

1.
The introduction of
something new

2.
A new idea, method,
or device : novelty

CHAPTER 13

A LEADER BECOMES A LEADER
BRIDGING TO NEW WORLDS

"The more we can focus our attention on the universe about us, the less taste we shall have for the destruction of our race. Wonder and humility are wholesome emotions, and they do not exist side by side with a lust for destruction."

—RACHEL CARSON
zoologist, author, and environmental visionary

BRIDGING TO NEW WORLDS

It was a hot summer's afternoon, and J. R. R. Tolkien's mind was wandering. In the summer of 1928, long before he became the world-renowned author of *The Lord of the Rings*, he was just making his name as a young professor in philology. He had made his business the exploration of words, but this time, he could not get through grading his students' final exam papers.

The piles of booklets, all answering the same set of questions, created a mind-numbing repetitiveness that left him woozy, like a prize fighter on wobbly legs. Students' handwritten ideas blurred before him. Suddenly, fortunately, there appeared a virgin set of pages in the middle of one student's examination booklet. Welcome relief came with the unexpected open space. Into the great space of empty lines and crisp white, his mind floated. And there, in the stillness of a professor's fertile summer imagination, stood a hobbit in a hole.

He looked at the hobbit. The hobbit looked at him. And he wrote down in the open lines a simple description of what his mind's eye saw. "One of the candidates had mercifully left one of the pages with no writing on it," he would recall years later, "which is the best thing that can possibly happen to an examiner. I wrote on it: 'In a hole in the ground there lived a hobbit.' Names always generate a story in my mind: eventually I thought I'd better find out what hobbits were like."

Finding out what hobbits were like became a life's journey for J. R. R. Tolkien. With vivid storytelling, he would lead readers into imagined places where epic battles of good versus evil were fought. Tolkien's achievement in creating Middle Earth was to imagine an entire world in astonishing detail—not only its geography and flora, but also its various races, along with their histories and mythologies, their languages and literature and music. Little wonder, then, that audiences around the world have developed a special bond with his characters.

Leaders who build bridges to new worlds begin as professors grading papers. They begin as young Native American teenage girls with names such as Sacagawea, who was unexpectedly called to join a band of experienced military explorers, and set out on the Lewis and Clark expedition. Their authority derives not from their title or position, but instead from their uncommon imagination and deep instinct. It's as if they carry with them a solitary faith that the places they find on the other side of our collective fears will deliver important new beauty, value, and meaning to those who follow behind.

They light their trails with a fire they have kindled by living lives of uncluttered passion. Such leaders chase the edges of new worlds with the energy of a girl named Helen Keller, who, lost to the world under the weight of extreme physical disabilities, muscled her way back to the mainland of community and social connectedness. Such leaders trek through uncharted territory, untouched by criticism that they are on quixotic misadventures, because their internal senses of direction are so bright. Experience has taught them that they are on the right track. Wrong turns only lead to better answers.

Helen Keller began life as a perfectly healthy infant, but fever and illness caused her to descend into a hellish prison of physical impairment. Blind and deaf from a young age, she was not able to perceive even that she existed as an individual until she was four years old. It was in her relationship with Annie Sullivan, whom she called "Teacher," that she found a way back to humanity from her darkness of isolation and terror. She left a world of utter solitude to journey to a world of society and civilization, where she would lead a revolution in the way people learn, interact, and overcome their limitations.

Her journey was Herculean. She describes in mythological terms the roadmaps she chose with her teacher: "Teacher, as I always called Anne Sullivan Macy, was with me, though unseen, and the Greek myths and poems which she had repeated to me as a child assumed a living reality. The climb up the Acropolis symbolized the difficulties Teacher and I had overcome together, and I was spiritually strengthened to ascend a metaphorical Acropolis in my work for the blind."

Historian Rhea Eliza Porter White strikes a similar note in her description of the Lewis and Clark expedition, a journey of epic proportions that led to a view so fresh and new that it commanded others to follow: "They drank from the Salmon, from the Snake and the Columbia rivers, built canoes that carried them down to the Columbia's mouth. On November 15th, 1805, they saw the shine of the Pacific…. After this, the expedition raised the Stars and Stripes above the great Pacific Ocean."

"No pessimist ever discovered the secrets of the stars,
or sailed to an uncharted land,
or opened a new heaven to the human spirit."

—HELEN KELLER
humanitarian and civil rights advocate

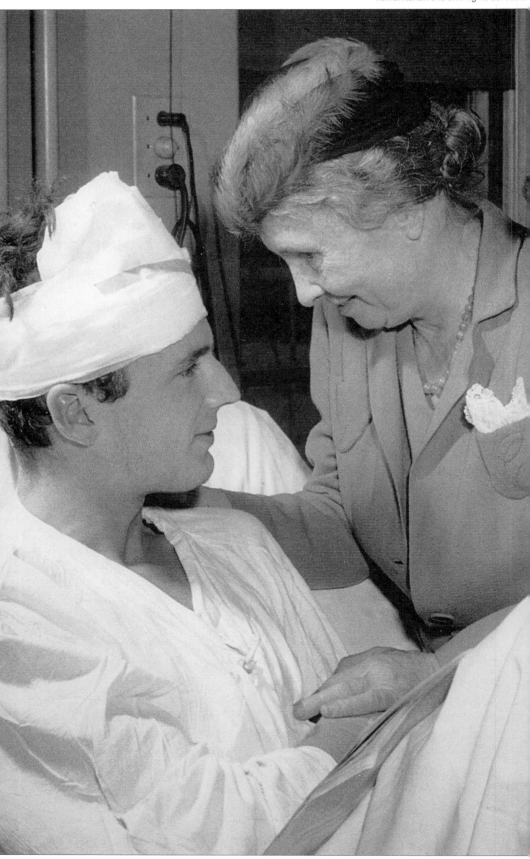

Helen Keller became a leader in darkness,
overcoming the isolation of disability to become a voice heard around the world.

No light. No sound. She lived in a darkness of silent desperation and terrifying isolation that enveloped her whole being. Close your eyes. Plug your ears, so that you can't hear anything. That was what existence was for Helen Keller.

SHE CREATED PATHWAYS FROM UTTER ISOLATION

She compared herself to a shipwrecked sea captain who has to learn a new language just to get back to society and the mainland. Roger Shattuck, who wrote the forward to the most comprehensive edition of her autobiography, *The Story of My Life*, placed her journey through disability "next to the epic of Odysseus finding his way home and to Columbus finding his way to the new world." She went from being a child–blind, deaf, and so isolated from the world around her that she would descend into depths of rage–to being a woman of such compassion, vision, intellectual stature, and personal achievement that world leaders sought her counsel, friendship, and affection.

One cannot imagine the horror and overwhelming sadness she confronted when she first realized she was so separate. She reports in her memoirs that it happened at five years old. She was standing between two close friends, feeling their lips and faces as they spoke to one another, when it dawned on her that there was an entire world of communication, connection, and meaning to which she didn't have a key.

The sea captain's journey back began at six, when a heroic teacher of exceptional vision and talent took Helen under her wing. Annie Sullivan helped steer her precocious student over the barrier reefs that seemed to be everywhere to a safe harbor that brought Helen fulfillment and joy. Helen observed, "Before my teacher came, I didn't know that I am." It was as if Odysseus had found a modern compass that could point the way to the warmth, intelligence, and meaning of the world. The two explorers used the only open channels they had–the young girl's hands, through which she could feel the world, and her mind, which could discern, systematize, and understand.

Annie Sullivan taught her to spell through a system of touches on the young girl's palm. She taught Helen to speak by having her touch the teacher's face, mouth, and throat, and then mimic the movements. She decided at the outset that treating her student as a normal child, and expecting others to do the same, would produce the best results. She wrote that her teacher moved her from "darkness into light," and from "isolation to friendship, companionship, knowledge, love." An inner voice told her on her teacher's arrival that "knowledge is love and light and vision." Before that, all the voice could muster in the dark hours of haunted separation was a solitary cry, "Light, give me light!"

Each step took enormous courage and steadfast will. Helen wrote: "I slip back many times, I fall, I stand still, I run against the edge of hidden obstacles, I lose my temper and find it again and keep it better, I trudge on, I gain a little, I feel encouraged, I get more eager and climb higher to begin to see the widening horizon. Every struggle is a victory." The victories combined to create a fascinating history. She described meeting Mark Twain: "I read from Mark Twain's lips one or two of his good stories…. I feel the twinkle of his eye in his handshake. Even while he utters his cynical wisdom in an indescribably droll voice, he makes you feel that his heart is a tender Iliad of human sympathy." Here, she experiences Niagara Falls for the first time: "I could hardly realize that it was water I felt rushing and plunging with impetuous fury at my feet. It seemed as if it were some living thing rushing on to some terrible fate."

In the end, she knew that her ultimate passage to the world was through other people. And, on some level, she sensed that that aspect of her made her more like everybody else than any other: "I try to make the light in others' eyes my sun, the music in others' ears my symphony, the smile on others' lips my happiness." In her lifetime, she became not only an icon for the disabled, but a testament to the power of the desire to know oneself and to be free.

1880
Helen Keller is born in Tuscumbia, Alabama, to Captain Arthur Henley Keller and Kate Adams Heller.

1881
At nineteen months old, she is afflicted with a severe, sudden, and mysterious fever. The fever spikes quickly, and then disappears just as fast. The trauma weakens the fragile child, and leaves her completely blind and deaf.

1886
After several horribly trying years, during which Helen descends into an abyss of isolation and frustration, her family is introduced to Dr. Alexander Graham Bell in Washington, D.C. Bell determines that Keller's physical condition is untreatable, but that she is an exceptionally intelligent girl, and recommends that she attend the Perkins Institute for the Blind in Watertown, Massachusetts.

1887
The Kellers contact the Perkins Institute, which recommends a young woman named Annie Sullivan to be Helen's personal teacher. Teacher and student set out on an extraordinary journey of healing, education, and self-discovery.

1900
Keller enrolls at Radcliffe College in Cambridge, Massachusetts. She will graduate cum laude in 1904.

1903
At twenty-three, Keller publishes *The Story of My Life*, an international success that is eventually translated into fifty languages. It marks the beginning of a successful writing career.

1907
At twenty-seven, Keller writes a pioneering article in the *Ladies Home Journal* that advocates early prevention of certain common causes of blindness among infants.

1909
Keller joins the suffragette movement, and becomes politically active.

1924
Keller begins a lifetime of advocacy work for organizations that support the advancement of the oppressed. She works as a spokesperson for the American Foundation for the Blind. She will donate money to the NAACP, act as an early supporter of the American Civil Liberties Union's efforts to advance the cause of freedom of speech, and work tirelessly to bring attention to the cause of the poor and the disadvantaged.

1936
Annie Sullivan dies at sixty-nine.

1961
Helen Keller suffers a stroke and retires to private life.

1968
She dies at the age of eighty-eight. Her legacy as a woman who has overcome extraordinary physical limitations to use her many gifts to advance the cause of disadvantaged people everywhere shines around the world for people to emulate.

Helen Keller overcame what some said were impossible odds to attend college at the age of twenty. Although she is an icon for the disabled, she also fought strenuously for the rights of the poor throughout her adult life.

"Ocean in view! O! The joy!"

—WILLIAM CLARK
journal entry, Lewis and Clark expedition, November 7th, 1805

29 USA

SACAGAWEA

Sacagawea became a leader in the American Northwest,
helping Lewis and Clark build a bridge to the Native American cultures
of the lands obtained through the Louisiana Purchase.

When the Lewis and Clark expedition left St. Louis in the spring of 1804 and journeyed up the Missouri River, there were just five million people living in the United States. Early in his administration, President Thomas Jefferson, a vigorous, visionary young leader, had conceived of an expedition to open the unknown territories in what was known at the time as the Northwest Corridor. He wanted his young country to appreciate the details of a vast wilderness that spread west to the Pacific Ocean, and to find a northwest passage to connect east to west by water. Lewis and Clark's mission was to "penetrate a country at least two thousand miles in width." In one breathtaking journey, they redrew in a people's imagination the map of what was possible. Over a two-year span, they conducted research on the land and its vegetation, and collected extraordinary stories of an uncharted wilderness rich in space, resources and beauty.

HER PASSION FOR THE OCEAN DROVE THE JOURNEY

The American experiment was ripe for such challenges. Vast, uncharted land spread to the west and north. After obtaining federal funding, President Jefferson assembled a team of thirty-one military men, one translator, and one Native American woman to open new worlds and journey into the great unknown.

The practical objective–to find a continuous river channel that could serve as a commercial passage from the East Coast to the West Coast–would not be accomplished, because there was not one to be found. But the Corps of Discovery journeyed eight thousand miles, into the history books, uncovering one of nature's great frontiers, and peacefully coexisting with the Native American cultures they met along the way. It is hard to say which achievement was greater.

Sacagawea was a teenager when the expedition began. (She came to the Lewis and Clark Expedition as the wife of its translator.) Six months into the grueling physical adventure, she gave birth to a baby boy. Where some might have blended into the territory, focusing on a tiny living cargo and simply withstanding the journey's physical hardships, she became for them an indispensable guide, translator, and lieutenant to the expedition's founders.

Where some lead conspicuously with formal authority and resources, Sacagawea led with a certain quiet sensibility, reaching extraordinary places and human moments with a gifted touch and ability to connect. She supported the expedition when the expedition needed her most. She played an instrumental role in the Corps of Discovery's mission, holding the Corps together and working with the Native American tribes with great diplomatic skill.

She was a woman of unusual strength and common sense, trading for horses when the expedition needed a means of crossing the mountains. She demonstrated poise under pressure. In one instance, she pulled critical instruments, logs, books, and maps back into a capsizing canoe, the loss of which would have proven catastrophic.

Sacagawea had a dream in her youth of seeing the Big Water, the Pacific Ocean. She achieved that dream for herself and a new nation that rose in the east and would find a second border on its western side. An historian at the U.S. Treasury said of her, "Without Sacagawea's navigational, diplomatic, and translating skills, the famous Lewis and Clark expedition would have perished." Sacagawea's role as a leader and an integral player in one of the great expeditions in recorded history resulted from her willingness to embrace the Corps of Discovery's pioneering spirit, and to find within it the culmination of her own life's journey. Captain William Clark would write her husband at the end of the journey, "Your woman who accompanied you that long dangerous and fatiguing route to the Pacific Ocean and back disserved [sic] a greater reward for her attention and services on that rout [sic] than we had in our power to give her." History has rewarded her with a special place in our collective memory.

SACAGAWEA'S LIFE

1787
It is believed that Sacagawea was born to a Shoshone chief and his wife in the area of the North American continent that is now the state of Idaho.

1800
Hitatsa Indians kidnap the thirteen-year-old Shoshone Indian girl Sacagawea and sell her four years later to French trapper Toussaint Charbonneau, who makes her his wife.

1803
President Thomas Jefferson solicits Congress to finance an exploration of the western part of the North American continent. He estimates that it will take a thousand years to settle such a large expanse of territory. The exploration costs Congress thirty-eight thousand dollars.

May 1804
The Lewis and Clark expedition sets off from Camp Dubois in what is now the state of Illinois "under a jentle brease" (according to William Clark's journals).

November 1804
The Lewis and Clark Corps of Discovery hires Toussaint Charbonneau and his wife, Sacagawea, to act as interpreters on what will be a twenty-eight-month expedition. Sacagawea is sixteen years old and six months pregnant.

February 1805
Sacagawea gives birth to a boy, Jean Baptiste, after a near-fatal labor. She survives with the help and support of William Clark.

April 1805
The Corps of Discovery begins its journey from the upper Missouri, with Sacagawea carrying her eight-week-old infant on a cradleboard. Sacagawea becomes a quietly influential leader. She is able to help the Corps read the landscapes, and instinctively knows how to navigate through difficult territories. Her expertise in indigenous foods and the ways of the North American Indian prove critical to the Corps's success.

January 1806
Sacagawea fulfills a personal dream of seeing the ocean when the Corps of Discovery reaches what is now the Oregon seacoast.

September 1806
The Corps of Discovery ends its expedition in St. Louis, and its members are hailed as national heroes.

1812
Sacagawea dies at Fort Clark at the age of twenty-five. William Clark takes custody of her orphaned son, Jean Baptiste, and her daughter, Lisette.

GLIMPSES OF YOUTH

At just thirteen, Sacagawea was kidnapped by the warring Hidatsus Indians from her home in what is now the state of Idaho. She would spend her adolescent years in the Western Territories, which became the state of North Dakota.

"Quite by accident, I have a very vivid child's view."

—J. R. R. TOLKIEN
university professor and ground-breaking author

J. R. R. Tolkien became a leade
imagining fantastic worlds from invented language

He was a shy man, a gentle man. He wrote the initial idea for his adventure masterpieces, *The Hobbit* and *The Lord of the Rings* trilogy, in the margins of a student's examination booklet. *The Lord of the Rings* would become his life's work, a magical epic that would explode onto bestseller lists around the world as a new staple of children's literature. A half-century later, the trilogy would become the foundation of one of the great Academy Award-winning epics in the history of film.

HE INVENTED A LANGUAGE
AND OPENED A DOOR TO A NEW WORLD

It was at Oxford in 1928, when he was thirty-six, quietly, in the company of his students and in the arms of a supportive, admiring university community, that he first realized he could make literary magic. He had been a young soldier in World War I, where the sight of soldiers dying in great waves of human carnage had traumatized him. The memories drove him to seek sanctuary in normalcy and steadiness–a rhythm and style of living that was rooted in meaning and his immediate neighborhood. Life in his university town healed him.

International acclaim came to J. R. R. Tolkien soon after the release of *The Hobbit* in 1936. To maintain his balance as an academic and author, the esteemed professor shunned the spotlight. Instead, he chose a path of peaceful study, close to the students, family, and friends that he had grown to love over the years at Oxford. It was this place that had inspired him, and it was from these surroundings that would come his vision of hobbits, sorcery and magic, Middle Earth and small villages.

His journey to writing began with his love of words. As a teenager, he enjoyed inventing new languages. As a professional academic, he built on that teenage love to become a philologist–one who studies words and their origins. He once explained how powerful words were to his approach to writing: "The invention of language is the foundation," he explained. "The stories were made…to provide a world for the language [rather] than the reverse. To me a name comes first and story followed." The first word from *The Lord of the Rings*, which he wrote in the column of that student's examination booklet, was "hobbit." It was a word that would change the shape of children's literature.

His close friend, C. S. Lewis, explained their shared philosophy when he said, "I like boredom." Ironic, of course, for authors whose works took young readers on rollercoaster rides of survival through an evil witch's endless, frozen winter, and a world at war with the very grandmaster of evil. But salvation in their stories lay in the hands of seemingly powerless hobbits and children, whose simple faith and desire for the warmth of the summer sun seemed to overwhelm the power of everything in their path.

The hobbit that he invented in the column of that student's exam essay was, in large part, the essence of who J. R. R. Tolkien was: "I am, in fact, a hobbit in all but size," he wrote. "I like gardens, trees, unmechanized farm lands. I smoke a pipe and like good, plain food–unrefrigerated–but I detest French cooking. I like–and even dare to wear, in these dull days–ornamental waist coats. I'm fond of mushrooms out of a field, have a very simple sense of humor (which even my most appreciative critics find tiresome). I go to bed late, and get up late, when possible."

His son, Michael Tolkien, majestically described his father's ultimate contribution: "To me, at least, there is nothing mysterious behind the scale and extent of the appeal of my father's writing; his genius has simply answered the call of people of any age or temperament most wearied by the ugliness, the speed, the shoddy values, the slick philosophies which have been given them as dreary substitutions for the beauty, the sense of mystery, excitement, heroism and joy without which the very soul of man begins to wither and die within him."

TOLKIEN'S LIFE

1892
J. R. R. "Ronald" Tolkien is born to Arthur and Mabel Tolkien. His father is a bank manager, and his mother, a former missionary in Zanzibar.

1892-1896
In South Africa, as a young child, Ronald is bitten by a tarantula and then by a snake. A local kidnaps him to show off the young English boy to his extended clan. He will leave the country with a deep sense of mystery, adventure, and danger that he will employ later in his life as a writer.

1896-1904
His mother is his first teacher, his confidante, and his protector after his father dies when Ronald is three years old. She transmits to him a love of words, but dies in 1904, when he is just twelve.

1915
Tolkien receives his bachelor's degree from Exeter College in Oxford, where he studies English and the classics.

1916
Ronald marries Edith Bratt, with whom he has been in love since they met at a boarding house when he was eighteen. The two will have four children together.

1925-1959
Tolkien serves as a professor at Oxford University, eventually becoming the Merton Professor of English Language and Literature.

1928
Professor Tolkien is grading students' examinations on a summer day, and writes on a page of one examination booklet, "In a hole in the ground, there lived a hobbit." The sentence sets the stage for his life's masterwork.

1940-1954
The scholar spends fifteen years writing *Lord of the Rings*, a trilogy that he completes in his spare time. He later explains that the books began as a linguistics exercise, but the story subsequently caught his fancy.

1960s
The story of the Ring enchants millions of readers, and becomes an international bestseller.

1965-1973
Even in his 70s, Tolkien never fully retires; instead, he focuses his energies on unfinished works such as *The Silmarillion.* He says at the end of his life, "A pen is to me as a beak is to a hen."

1973
J. R. R. Tolkien dies at the age of eighty-one. The Ring trilogy will go on to become an Academy Award-winning film, and to inspire new generations with his story of good battling evil.

GLIMPSES OF YOUTH

J. R. R. Tolkien invented languages during his teen years. His bestselling *Lord of the Rings* depended on his ability to use the invention of new languages as a springboard for the creation of stories.

"Her memory of people is remarkable.
She remembers the grasp of fingers she has held before,
all the characteristic tightening of the muscles that make
one person's handshake different from that of another."

—ANNIE SULLIVAN
editor, *The Story of My Life*

"Clark saw Sacagawea,
who was with her husband 100 yards ahead,
begin to dance and show every mark of the most extravagant joy,
turning round him and pointing to several Indians, whom he now saw
advancing on horseback, sucking her fingers to indicate
that they were of her native tribe.

She came into the tent, sat down, and was beginning to interpret,
when in the person of Cameahwait she recognized her brother [after many
years' separation]; She instantly jumped up, and ran and embraced him,
throwing over him her blanket and weeping profusely."

—MERIWETHER LEWIS
journal entry, August 17th, 1805

BRIDGING TO NEW WORLDS

"[J. R. R. Tolkien] stands as a unique figure in literature.
While drawing inspiration from the style and mode of Celtic, Norse,
and Teutonic folklore…he revived…after a thousand years' lapse, the
role of epic minstrel; took up again, to popular acclaim in the
Twentieth Century, the immemorial theme of the Quest: the heroic
attempt of puny mortals to resolve the age long
cosmic conflict of good and evil."

—DANIEL GROTTA
The Biography of J. R. R. Tolkien: Architect of Middle Earth

dis·ci·pline

1.
Training expected to
produce a specific
character or pattern of
behavior, especially
training that produces
moral or
mental improvement

2.
Self-control

good will

1.
An attitude of kindness
or friendliness;
benevolence

2.
Cheerful acquiescence
or willingness

3.
A good relationship, as
a nation with other
nations

worlds

1.
The creative
imagination;
unrestrained fancy

2.
Fiction characterized
by highly fanciful or
supernatural elements

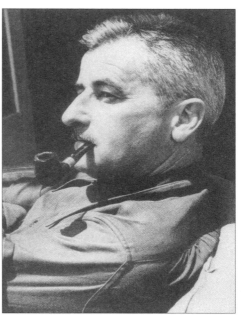

part 2

THE QUALITIES OF LEADERSHIP
A TRIBUTE
IN PHOTOGRAPHS

"You cannot hope to build a better world
without improving the individuals. To that end
each of us must work for his own improvement, and,
at the same time, share a general responsibility
for all humanity."

—MARIE CURIE

"There can be hope only
for a society which acts as one big family,
and not as many separate ones."

—ANWAR SADAT
former president of Egypt

LEADERS inspire hope.

On September 18th, 1978, U.S. President Jimmy Carter announced an historic peace agreement between Prime Minister Menachem Begin of Israel and President Anwar Sadat of Egypt. It was the first of its kind and would come to be known as the Camp David Accords.

A LEADER BECOMES A LEADER

"Unless we use the weapons of the spirit,…
men will go on fighting, and often from the highest
motives, believing that they are fighting defensive wars
for justice and in self-defense against present
or future aggression."

—DOROTHY DAY
founder of the Catholic Worker Movement

**LEADERS are
good with other people.**

Dorothy Day was the founder
of the Catholic Worker
Movement, whose goal is to
alleviate the problems of the
poor and suffering. The
movement has fostered a
national newspaper and one
hundred and thirty-four
communities that provide
emergency food, shelter, and
supplies.

"A good organizer has to work hard and long.
There are no shortcuts. You just keep talking to people,
working with them, sharing, exchanging,
and they come along."

—CÉSAR CHÁVEZ

THE FLEXIBILITY OF
MIKHAIL GORBACHEV
1921-

"We need a revolution of the mind."

—MIKHAIL GORBACHEV
former president of the Soviet Union

**LEADERS are flexible
in the worst circumstances.**

Mikhail Gorbachev was president of the Soviet Union from 1989 to 1991. His vision of a peaceful and more open society set the stage for a new era in world stability and politics.

"He has decided that he would risk his power in order to save his reforms, rather than risk his reforms and save his power."

—RICHARD NIXON
former president of the United States,
speaking of Gorbachev

A LEADER BECOMES A LEADER

"Don't be afraid to make a mistake.
But make sure you don't
make the same mistake twice."

–AKIO MORITA
cofounder of Sony Corporation

**LEADERS are
experts in their fields,
reliable, and down-to-earth.**

Akio Morita was the cofounder of the Sony Corporation. Bringing to market dramatic technical innovations such as the first video recorder and transistor television, he made his mark, championing humility as an important hallmark of business leadership.

A LEADER BECOMES A LEADER

"Mr. Gorbachev, tear down this wall!"

—RONALD REAGAN
40th president of the United States, at the Berlin Wall on June 12, 1987

LEADERS can be morally persuasive.

The Iron Curtain divided Europe from 1961 to 1989, and was a stark symbol of the Cold War. Moral suasion and leadership, including Pope John Paul II's dramatic visit to Poland in 1979 and United States President Ronald Reagan's powerful speech at the wall in 1987, coalesced with economic realities in the Soviet Union to finally bring the wall down.

"They knew how to deal with political pressure, but they didn't know what to do with moral pressure."

—A VATICAN OFFICIAL
to the *Chicago Tribune*, 1992

"Each time a man stands up for an ideal,
or acts to improve the lot of others…he sends forth a
tiny ripple of hope, and crossing each other from a
million different centers of energy and daring,
those ripples build a current which can sweep down the
mightiest walls of oppression and resistance."

–ROBERT F. KENNEDY
United States senator

LEADERS can
be very charismatic.

Robert F. Kennedy was attorney general of the United States from 1961 to 1963. His brazen belief in the power of fairness, hard work, and change marked the 1960s, and continues to resonate for people around the world who admire his courage and vision.

"One knows from life that we exist for other people–
first for all those upon whose smiles and well-being our
own happiness is wholly dependent, and then for the
many, unknown to us, to whose destinies
we are bound by the ties of sympathy."

–ALBERT EINSTEIN

"Morale is the state of mind. It is steadfastness and courage and hope. It is confidence and zeal and loyalty. It is élan, esprit de corps and determination."

–GENERAL GEORGE C. MARSHALL
United States secretary of state

LEADERS have command presence.

George Marshall was secretary of state under President Harry Truman from 1947 to 1950. By securing billions of dollars from his government to rebuild European countries decimated by World War II, he inspired a brotherhood among nations that resonates to the present when people say the words "Marshall Plan."

"He will receive the Nobel Peace Prize today,
because he...has become a witness for truth and justice.
From the abyss of the death camps he has come as a
messenger to mankind–not with a message of hate and
revenge, but with one of brotherhood and atonement.
He has become a powerful spokesman for the view of
mankind and the unlimited humanity which is, at all
times, the basis of a lasting peace. Elie Wiesel is not
only the man who survived–he is also the spirit which
has conquered. In him we see a man who has climbed
from utter humiliation to become one of our most
important spiritual leaders and guides.

I doubt whether any other individual, through the use
of such quiet speech, has achieved more or been more
widely heard. The words are not big, and the voice
which speaks them is low. It is a voice of peace we hear.
But the power is intense. Truly, the little spark will not
be put out, but will become a burning torch for our
common belief in the future. Truly, prisoner number
A7713 has become a human being once again–
a human being dedicated to humanity."

–from the citation for the 1986 Nobel Peace Prize

"Sometimes we must interfere.
When human lives are endangered, when human
dignity is in jeopardy, national borders and sensitivities
become irrelevant. Whenever men or women are
persecuted because of their race, religion, or political
views, that place must–at that moment–
become the center of the universe."

–ELIE WIESEL
Noble Peace laureate

**LEADERS tap wells of inner
strength and rise to the
most difficult challenges.**

When he was fifteen years
old, Elie Wiesel survived one
of the worst genocides in
human history: ten million
people, including most of his
immediate family, were sum-
marily executed by a fascist
regime during World War II.
Since then, he has spent a
lifetime serving humanity as
a witness to history, leading
readers into the darkest
dimensions of human nature.
"Forget," they told the
prisoners in the death camps.
Elie Wiesel chose, instead, to
remember.

THE SELF-CONFIDENCE OF
DUKE ELLINGTON

1899-1974

"My biggest kick in music–
playing or writing–is when I have a problem.
Without a problem to solve,
how much interest do you take
in anything?"

–DUKE ELLINGTON
bandleader and composer

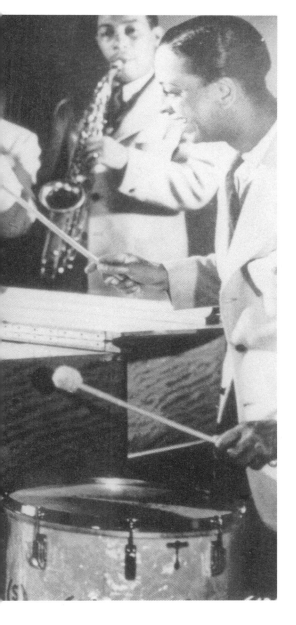

LEADERS are self-confident.

Edward Kennedy Ellington, "Duke" to all the world, was one of the great composers of the twentieth century. He wrote hundreds of powerful compositions, including the well-known "Take the 'A' Train" and "Satin Doll."

"I tell them I don't have any formula for ousting
a dictator or building democracy. All I can suggest
is to forget about yourself and just think of your people.
It's always the people who make things happen."

–CORAZON AQUINO
former president of the Philippines

**LEADERS have force
of personality from the very
person they have become.**

Corazon Aquino became the
president of the Republic of
the Philippines, replacing
her husband just a few years
after he was assassinated. A
politically informed mother
of five, she navigated the
unstable waters of a reeling
body politic with an unwa-
vering commitment to non-
violence and democratic
principles. She served from
1986 to 1992.

A LEADER BECOMES A LEADER

"I believe that man will not merely endure;
he will prevail. He is immortal, not because he alone
among creatures has an inexhaustible voice, but because
he has a soul, a spirit capable of compassion and
sacrifice and endurance.
The poet's, the writer's duty is to write about these
things. It is his privilege to help man endure by lifting
his heart, by reminding him of the courage and honor
and hope and pride and compassion and pity and
sacrifice which have been the glory of his past.
The poet's voice need not simply be the record of man,
it can be one of the props, the pillars to help
him endure and prevail."

—WILLIAM FAULKNER
accepting the Nobel Prize for Literature in Stockholm, Sweden,
December 10, 1950

**LEADERS have wisdom,
foresight, and intelligence.**

William Faulkner reinvented
the way novels are written,
capturing truths of the heart
in a fictional county named
Yoknapatawpha, where the
past mixed with the present,
and the dead and the living
spoke to one another.

"Negative emotions are always the true enemy,
a factor that has to be overcome and eliminated.
And it is only by applying methods
for training the mind that these negative emotions
can be dispelled and eliminated."

—HIS HOLINESS THE DALAI LAMA
leader of Tibet

LEADERS have unceasing optimism.

The current Dalai Lama is the fourteenth Dalai Lama to lead Tibet. Exiled since 1959, he has sought a peaceful solution that will enable Tibet to continue as an independent country with its rich history and culture intact, despite ongoing aggression from neighboring China.

THE TEAM PLAY OF
EDSON ARANTES DO NASCIMENTO 'PELÉ'

"Every kid around the world who plays soccer
wants to be Pelé. I have a great responsibility
to show them not just how to be like a soccer player,
but how to be like a man."

−PELÉ
professional soccer player

LEADERS strive
for a sense of team play.

Born Edson Arantes do Nascimento, "Pelé", as the world came to know him, became one of the greatest soccer players ever to play the game. He lead Brazil to two World Cup championships. At just 17 years old, Pelé made his World Cup début, scoring the all-important solo goal in a 1-0 shutout of the Soviet Union.

A LEADER BECOMES A LEADER

"Just don't give up trying to do
what you really want to do. Where there is
love and inspiration, I don't think
you can go wrong."

–ELLA FITZGERALD
jazz vocalist and international icon

LEADERS work to bring integrity to everything they do.

Ella Fitzgerald's first appearances were as a gospel singer in her father's church. She began singing in nightclubs as a teenager. Frank Sinatra called her "my all-time favorite." From her première at the Apollo Theater at just sixteen years old, she became an international icon–an embodiment of all things jazz. Collaborators and listeners around the world adored her for her sense of playfulness, powerful energy, three-octave range–and that voice. For decades, it seemed to dance across the moonlit terrace of every jazz-inspired evening.

A LEADER BECOMES A LEADER

"Look, in a crisis you have to be optimistic. When I said the spirit of the city would be stronger, I didn't know that. I just hoped it. There are parts of you that say, 'Maybe we're not going to get through this.' You don't listen to them."

—RUDOLPH GUILIANI
former mayor of New York City

LEADERS have an unusual ability to inspire and motivate others.

Rudolph Giuliani was the mayor of New York City from 1993 to 2001. During his tenure, the city became a model for urban turn-arounds, with crime rates and unemployment dropping dramatically. But he may best be remembered by history for his healing presence, leading the city and the world in the days and weeks after September 11th, 2001.

"After midnight the moon set and I was alone with the stars. I have often said that the lure of flying is the lure of beauty, and I need no other flight to convince me that the reason flyers fly, whether they know it or not, is the aesthetic appeal of flying."

—AMELIA EARHART
aviation pioneer

LEADERS are daring.

In 1937, Amelia Earhart became the first woman in history to fly across the Pacific Ocean. She died attempting the first around-the-world flight. Her plane disappeared into the ocean, but her legacy holds a prominent place in the lore of the twentieth century.

"Ladies and gentlemen, there are moments
in the lives of nations and peoples when it is incumbent
upon those known for their wisdom and clarity of
vision to survey the problem, with all its complexities
and vain memories, in a
bold drive toward new horizons."

—ANWAR SADAT

LEADERS have the ability to navigate the most difficult conflicts.

Anwar Sadat was president of Egypt from 1970 until 1981, when he was assassinated by political radicals. With a combination of tough-minded negotiating tactics and fidelity to his faith, he signed the historic Camp David Accords with Israel's Menachem Begin in 1978, demonstrating to the world a better way of resolving conflict in the Middle East. "Today we agree to live with you in permanent peace and justice," he said.

"He who cannot change the very fabric of his thought
will never be able to change reality, and will never,
therefore, make any progress."

—ANWAR SADAT

A LEADER BECOMES A LEADER

"The thing that lies at the foundation of positive change, the way I see it, is service to a fellow human being."

—LECH WALESA
leader of the workers' freedom movement in Poland

LEADERS have the ability to take initiative that can exceed everyday constraints.

Lech Walesa was employed as an electrician in the shipyards of Gdansk when he began organizing union workers, for which he was detained by Polish authorities. He eventually led shipyard strikes and rose to become the leader of the trade union Solidarity, which was a cornerstone in the fight for freedom for workers across Eastern Europe.

1869-1948

"As human beings,
our greatness lies not so much in being able
to remake the world–that is the myth of the
atomic age–as in being able to
remake ourselves."

–MOHANDAS GANDHI

**LEADERS are steady
even under extreme pressure.**

Mohandas Gandhi helped liberate millions by leading the freedom fight in South Africa and then India. Leaders from Martin Luther King, Jr., to Nelson Mandela have studied, implemented, and adapted his teachings of nonviolent resistance.

"The moment we begin to fear
the opinions of others and hesitate to tell the truth that
is in us…the divine floods of light and life no longer
flow into our souls."

–ELIZABETH CADY STANTON,
organizer and writer for the suffragette movement

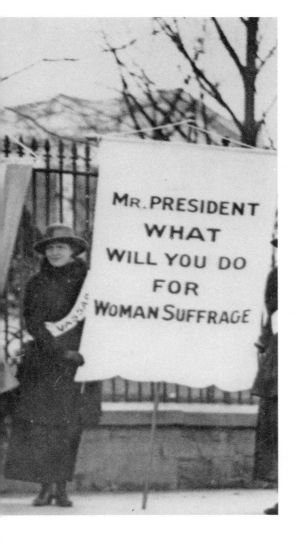

**GROUPS of people lead
when they unite in a
common purpose.**

"Hundreds of women gave the accumulated possibilities of an entire lifetime, thousands gave years of their lives, hundreds of thousands gave constant interest and such aid as they could. It was a continuous, seemingly endless chain of activity. Young suffragists who helped forge the last links in that chain were not born when it began. Old suffragists who forged the first links were dead when it ended."

**–CARRIE CHAPMAN CATT,
NETTIE ROGERS SHULER**
*Woman Suffrage and Politics: The Inner
Story of the Suffragette Movement*

"I've missed more than nine thousand shots in my career. I've lost almost three hundred games. Twenty-six times, I've been trusted to take the game winning shot and missed. I've failed over and over and over again in my life. And that is why I succeed."

–MICHAEL JORDAN
professional basketball player

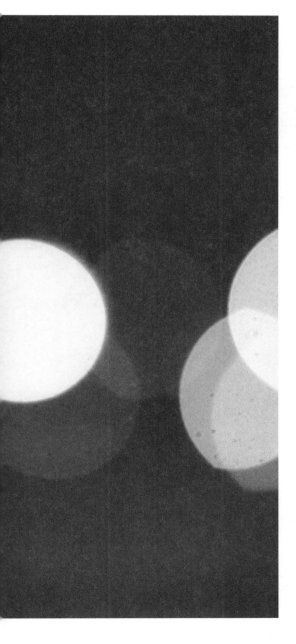

LEADERS act decisively, but also know when to rest, regroup, and assess the situation.

Michael Jordan is considered by many the greatest professional basketball player ever to play the game. As a member of the Chicago Bulls, he twice led the team to three consecutive NBA Championships (six total titles), and was the regular season Most Valuable Player five times.

A LEADER BECOMES A LEADER

"If you apply reason and logic
to this career of mine,
you're not going to get very far....
The journey has been incredible from its beginning."

–SIDNEY POITIER
first African-American actor to win an Academy Award for Best Actor

LEADERS are noble.

Sidney Poitier was one of the most compelling actors of the 1960s. He won the Academy Award for Best Actor, and became the number-one box office draw in 1967 for *Guess Who's Coming to Dinner*, a movie that shook audiences for its open discussion of interracial relationships.

1913-1970

"Individual commitment to a group effort–
that is what makes a team work,
a company work, a society work, a civilization work."

–VINCE LOMBARDI
championship NFL football coach and general manager

LEADERS are able to attract the best talent, and inspire teamwork in the people around them.

Vince Lombardi was general manager and head coach of the Green Bay Packers from 1958-1967. He built one of the great sports dynasties in professional sports, winning six NFL championships and two Super Bowls.

"The way they behave as people
is more important than their playing skills."

–VINCE LOMBARDI

A LEADER BECOMES A LEADER

"The only thing we have to fear,
is fear itself."

–FRANKLIN DELANO ROOSEVELT
32nd president of the United States

**LEADERS know their
limitations and work with
others who are strong
where they are weak.**

Franklin Delano Roosevelt led
the American people out of
an international economic
depression, and through a
world war that threatened
the security of free people
everywhere.

THE STEADY HAND OF
JOHN F. KENNEDY

1917-1963

"In the long history of the world,
only a few generations
have been granted the role of defending freedom
in its hour of maximum responsibility....
I welcome it."

—JOHN FITZGERALD KENNEDY
35th president of the United States

**All leaders are tested;
they succeed through patience,
perseverance, and discipline.**

In the fall of 1962, John F. Kennedy's government discovered nuclear missiles in Cuba that could destroy millions of people in a matter of minutes. The ensuing standoff with the Soviet Union was eventually resolved through strategy, patience, focus, nerve, a naval blockade, and a back-channel communication to Soviet Premier Nikita Khrushchev.

part 3

A LEADER BECOMES A LEADER
CONCLUSION

"We need leaders of inspired idealism, leaders to whom are granted great visions, who dream greatly and strive to make their dreams come true: who can kindle the people with the fire from their own burning souls."

—THEODORE ROOSEVELT
26th president of the United States

A LEADER BECOMES A LEADER
CONCLUSION

In retelling these profound stories, I found that courage in leadership has defined our collective story best when it speaks for itself–in the visions and the fears; in the triumphs and the tragedies; in the voices, the discoveries, and the days in which these leaders served the people around them, and helped lift a common culture to higher ground.

One can devise formulas for becoming a leader. I have preferred to let the process show itself–in the faces and the names, in the dreams and the places, and in the power, the failings, the stillness, and the suffering of a group of individuals who dared to reach outside the status quo to find a place of greater civilization.

César Chávez never made more than six thousand dollars a year. Nelson Mandela did not provide a retirement fund for himself or his family during those twenty-seven years in prison. But through their actions and words, both provided shelter and security, freedom and life, for hundreds of thousands who lived within the reach of the warm rays of the spirit of their self-sacrifice, and their visionary examples. Through leadership, they helped relight the power of the universal civilizing principles by which they lived. Through leadership, they helped ignite in the hearts and minds of those who followed their paths a desire to find opportunities to lead again and again.

From Birmingham to Calcutta, from Montreal to Durban, the leaders featured here developed the capacity to inspire in a people, and in themselves, a vision of a better life. They became what they did by magnifying in themselves a set of universal values, instincts, and skills for leadership that often go underestimated or unrecognized when people settle for less. They became what they did by recognizing that their place in life was important to the human condition, and by making that place one of strength, civility, and inspiration. They spent a currency called faith, rising to their moments on visions that were solitary, new, and, at first, as untested as the early flying machines that adventurers like the Wright Brothers used to break free of the confines of earth and take flight.

From the Yosemite of Ansel Adams to the isolation of Helen Keller, from the exodus of Bob Marley to the freedom of Aung San Suu Kyi, these leaders shine as examples of what human beings can be when they tap the hidden energies of a world connected; and when, sometimes, in the reflection and resonance of the collective human imagination, they help us all touch the light of one common humanity.

A LEADER BECOMES A LEADER

"Leadership is not so much about technique and methods as it is about opening the heart. Leadership is about inspiration– of oneself and of others.

"Great leadership is about human experiences, not processes. Leadership is not a formula or a program, it is a human activity that comes from the heart and considers the hearts of others. It is an attitude, not a routine.

"More than anything else today, followers believe they are part of a system, a process that lacks heart. If there is one thing a leader can do to connect… at a human… level, it is to become engaged… fully, to share experiences and emotions, and to set aside the processes of leadership we have learned by rote."

–LANCE SECRETAN
leadership consultant

"Train your eyes, ears, hands, and mind–all your faculties–in the faithful doing of your chosen work. Use it as a tool to develop the strong points of your character and to eliminate the weak ones.

"Character is greater than any career. Each faculty must be educated, and any deficiency in its training will appear in whatever you do. The hand must be educated to be graceful, steady, and strong. The eye

conclusion

must be educated to be alert, discriminating, and microscopic. The heart must be educated to be tender, sympathetic, and true. The memory must be drilled for years in accuracy, retention, and comprehensiveness....

"Resolve that your life's work shall be a masterpiece. No matter whether it is farming, lawmaking, or home-building, let it be a masterpiece. Thoroughness leads to quality. And thoroughness is at the foundation of all success–your own inner success in character building, and your outward success in the world of progress....

"It is perfectly possible to exalt the most ordinary business by bringing to it the spirit of a master. The trouble with us is that we drop into a humdrum existence and do our work mechanically, with no heart, no vim, and no purpose. We do not learn the fine art of living for growth, for mind and soul expansion. We just exist....

"The habit of always choosing the highest within your reach, of doing the best thing possible under the circumstances, cannot be overestimated. Unconsciously you grow stronger and more effective, not only along the line of your career, but also along every line of character and achievement.

"If you always try to do the right thing in every place and under every circumstance, the very best you know; if you form the life habit of doing everything to a finish; if you stamp the trademark of excellence on everything that goes through your hands; if you keep your thought pure and high, your mind open and generous, fearless and honest; if you keep your ideals looking upward, you will be a marked person. Every day of your life will add a new chapter of improvement to your character. You will be a success in every sense of the word.

"There is in all of us a sleeping lion. It is just a question of arousing it."

–from **"LET EXCELLENCE BE YOUR TRADEMARK"**
by Ken Shelton and the editors of *Success* magazine,
based on the writings of Swett Marden (1850-1924)

A LEADER BECOMES A LEADER

conclusion

"The credit belongs to the man
who is actually in the arena, whose face is marred
by dust and sweat...who knows the great
enthusiasms, the great devotions and spends
himself in a worthy cause; who at best, if he wins,
knows the thrills of high achievement, and, if he
fails, at least fails daring greatly, so that his place
shall never be with those cold and timid souls who
know neither victory or defeat."

–JOHN F. KENNEDY
quoting Theodore Roosevelt, New York City, December 5th, 1961

ALBERT EINSTEIN

"Do not go
where the path may lead.
Go instead where there
is no path…
and leave a trail."

–RALPH WALDO EMERSON
transcendentalist, author, and friend of Henry David Thoreau

about the AUTHOR

Kevin Sheehan has had a distinguished career as an author, producer, and award-winning entrepreneur. For twenty years, he has produced recordings, films, books, software, and retail environments that have helped change the way people manage and view culture, and the way they shape and share inspiration.

He is the founder of Hear Music, now Starbucks Hear Music ("The Sound of Starbucks"). Widely heralded for its important innovations, the company has played a unique role in redefining music retail for almost two decades. *Elle* magazine likened a visit to the original store to "dying and going to music heaven." National Public Radio wondered how the experience did not exist before 1992.

Sheehan has had the good fortune to work with a variety of creative partners, including the internationally acclaimed dance troupe La La Human Steps of Montreal, Canada, and the Haley House Men's Shelter of Boston, Massachusetts, which has developed an innovative bakery and café to train and re-employ people who have fallen on hard times.

Sheehan is currently active in real estate and publishing in Massachusetts, and serves as a consultant to several nonprofit organizations.

BOOKS

ADAMS, ANSEL.
Ansel Adams: An Autobiography.
Trust Bulfinch,1985.

BLACK, CONRAD.
Franklin Delano Roosevelt: Champion of Freedom. Public Affairs, 2003.

BRIGHT, RANDY.
Disneyland: Inside Story. Harry N. Abrams, 1987.

CAMERON, JULIA.
The Artist's Way. 10th Anniversary ed. Jeremy P. Tarcher, 2002.

CANFIELD, JACK.
The Success Principles: How to Get from Where You Are to Where You Want to Be.
HarperCollins, 2005.

CARSON, CLAYBORNE.
The Eyes on the Prize: Civil Rights Reader; Documents, Speeches, and Firsthand Accounts from the Black Freedom Struggle, 1954-1990.
Reprint, Penguin Books, 1991.

CARSON, RACHEL.
Silent Spring. 40th Anniversary ed. Mariner Books, 2002.

CARSON, RACHEL.
The Sea Around Us. Oxford University Press, 1991.

CARPENTER, HUMPHREY.
J. R. R. Tolkien: A Biography. Houghton Mifflin, 2000.

COLEMAN, RAY.
Lennon: The Definitive Biography. rev. ed.
Perennial, 1992.

COUSINS, NORMAN.
Dr. Schweitzer of Lambaréné. Greenwood Press,1973.

DAVIES, PETER, AND WILLIAM MORRIS, *et al.*
The American Heritage Dictionary of the English Language. 4th ed. Houghton Mifflin, 2000.

EASWARAN, EKNATH.
Gandhi the Man: The Story of his Transformation.
3rd ed. Nilgiri Press, 1997.

EDELMAN, MARIAN WRIGHT.
The Measure of Our Success: Letters To My Children and Yours. Reprint, Perennial Currents, 1993.

ELIOT, T. S.
Four Quartets. Harvest Books, 1968.

FERRIS, SUSAN AND RICARDO SANDOVAL.
The Fight in the Fields: César Chávez and the Farm Workers Movement. Harvest Books, 1998.

FREEDMAN, RUSSELL.
Martha Graham: A Dancer's Life.
Clarion Books, 1998.

FULLER, MILLARD AND DIANE SCOTT.
No More Shacks!: The Daring Vision of Habitat for Humanity. Thomas Nelson, 1996.

GANDHI, MAHATMA.
The Penguin Gandhi Reader. Penguin Books, 1995.

GANDHI, MAHATMA, AND JOHN DEAR.
Mohandas Gandhi: Essential Writings.
Orbis Books, 2002.

GOLDSMITH, BARBARA.
Obsessive Genius. W. W. Norton, 2005.

GOODWIN, DORIS KEARNS.
No Ordinary Time: Franklin and Eleanor Roosevelt; The Home Front in World War II.
Reprint, Simon & Schuster, 1995.

GRAHAM, KATHARINE.
Personal History. Vintage, 1998.

GREENE, RICHARD AND KATHERINE.
Inside the Dream: The Personal Story of Walt Disney. Disney Editions, 2001.

GROTTA, DANIEL, GREG HILDEBRANDT, AND TIM HILDEBRANDT.
J. R. R. Tolkien: Architect of Middle Earth.
Running Press Book Publishers, 2001.

HALBERSTAM, DAVID.
Playing for Keeps: Michael Jordan and the World He Made. Broadway, 2000.

HEINZ, THOMAS A.
The Vision of Frank Lloyd Wright.
Book Sales, 2000.

HENTOFF, NAT.
Listen to the Stories: Nat Hentoff on Jazz and Country Music. Da Capo, 2000.

HUNSAKER, JOYCE BADGLEY.
Sacagawea Speaks: Beyond the Shining Mountains with Lewis and Clark. Falcon, 2001.

JORDAN, MICHAEL.
I Can't Accept Not Trying. HarperCollins, 1994.

KELLER, HELEN.
The Story of My Life. Reprint, Bantam Books, 1991.

KYI AUNG SAN SUU.
Freedom from Fear and Other Writings.
rev. ed. Penguin Books, 1995.

LENNON, CYNTHIA.
John. Crown, 2005.

LOREN, ERIC.
Disney Discourse: Producing the Magic Kingdom.
AFI Film Readers. Smoodin Routledge, 1994.

LOURIE, PETER.
On the Trail of Sacagawea. Boyds Mills, 2001.

MANCHESTER, WILLIAM.
The Last Lion: Winston Spencer Churchill; Visions of Glory, 1874-1932. Reprint, Delta,1984.

MANDELA, NELSON.
Long Walk to Freedom: The Autobiography of Nelson Mandela. Back Bay Books, 1995.

MANDELA, NELSON.
Long Walk to Freedom. Little Brown, 1994.

MAZO, JOSEPH H.
Prime Movers: The Makers of Modern Dance in America. William Morrow, 1977.

MCELVAINE, ROBERT.
The Great Depression: America 1929-1941.
Three Rivers, 1993.

MUGGERIDGE, MALCOLM.
Something Beautiful for God.
Reprint, Harper San Francisco, 1986.

PASACHOFF, NAOMI.
Marie Curie and the Science of Radioactivity.
Oxford University Press, 1997.

PFLAUM, ROSALYND.
Grand Obsession: Madame Curie and Her World. Doubleday, 1989.

ROBERTS, SELENA.
A Necessary Spectacle: Billie Jean King, Bobby Riggs, and the Tennis Match that Leveled the Game. Crown, 2005.

ROOSEVELT, ELEANOR.
Tomorrow is Now. HarperCollins, 1966.

ROOSEVELT, ELLIOT AND JAMES BROUGH.
Mother R: Eleanor Roosevelt's Untold Story.
Putnam, 1977.

ROSAFORTE, TIM.
Raising the Bar: The Championship Years of Tiger Woods. St. Martin's Griffin, 2002.

SCHILPP, P.A.
Albert Einstein: Philosopher-Scientist.
Open Court, 1988.

BOOKS *continued*

SEAVER, GEORGE.
Albert Schweitzer: The Man and His Mind.
Black, 1969.

SHAW, GEORGE BERNARD.
Back to Methuselah. Oxford University Press, 1947.

SHEFF, DAVID.
All We Are Saying: The Last Major Interview with John Lennon and Yoko Ono.
St. Martin's Griffin, 2000.

SHEPARD, KRIS AND CLAYBORNE CARSON.
A Call to Conscience: The Landmark Speeches of Dr. Martin Luther King, Jr. Warner Books, 2001.

SHILTS, RANDY.
The Mayor of Castro Street: The Life and Times of Harvey Milk. St. Martin's, 1982.

STONE, IRVING. *The Agony and the Ecstasy: A Biographical Novel of Michelangelo.*
NAL Trade, 2004.

TAFEL, EDGAR.
Years with Frank Lloyd Wright. Peter Smith, 1985.

TAFEL, EDGAR.
Apprentice to Genius. McGraw-Hill, 1979.

THOMAS, BENJAMIN P.
Abraham Lincoln: A Biography. Alfred A. Knopf, 1968.

TERESA, MOTHER AND JOSE LUIS GONZALEZ-BALADO.
Mother Teresa: In My Own Words.
Gramercy Books, 1997.

TYGIEL, JULES.
Baseball's Great Experiment: Jackie Robinson and His Legacy. Oxford University Press,
Expedition, 1997.

WALLACE, JAMES AND JIM ERICKSON.
Hard Drive: Bill Gates and the Making of the Microsoft Empire. Reprint, Harper Business,1993.

WARD, GEOFFREY C., AND KEN BURNS.
Jazz: A History of America's Music.
Alfred A. Knopf, 2000.

WASSERMAN, JACK.
Leonardo da Vinci (Masters of Art).
Harry N. Abrams, 1984.

WENNER, JANN S., AND JOHN LENNON.
Lennon Remembers. W.W. Norton, 2001.

WHITE, TIMOTHY.
Catch a Fire: The Life of Bob Marley.
Reprint, Owl Books, 1998.

BROADCASTS

"All Things Considered." Bob Boilen. NPR Radio,
Washington, D.C. April 30, 2003.

"Footprints on the Moon." Geoffrey Burchfield and
Harvey Broadbent. Quantum. ABC, Australia. 1999.

"To The Moon." Paula S. Apsell. Nova. PBS, Boston. 1999.

**"The Fight in the Fields: César Chávez and the Farm
Workers Struggle."** Rick Tejada-Flores and Ray Telles.
Independent Television Service. ITVS, San Francisco. 1997.

FILMS

The Adventurers: Neil Armstrong. PBS Video.
Café Productions, 1997.

Mandela: Son of Africa, Father of a Nation.
Palm Pictures, 1997.

Thirteen Days. New Line Home Entertainment, 2000.

The Times of Harvey Milk. New Yorker Video, 2004.

INTERNET ARTICLES

"A Class Of One." Public Broadcasting Service.
February 18, 1997.
http://www.pbs.org/newshour/bb/race_relations/
jan-june97/bridges_2-18.html.

"A Science Odyssey: People and Discoveries."
Public Broadcasting Service. WGBH Interactive
Media. January 16, 2003.
http://www.pbs.org/wgbh/aso/databank/entries/
btcars.html.

"Bobby Riggs vs. Billie Jean King." PageWise.
February 20, 2003.
http://ok.essortment.com/billiejeanking_rvwa.html.

**"The Brandt Equation: 21st Century Blueprint for the
New Global Economy."** Global Negotiations.
June 12, 2005. Brandt21forum.info.
http://www.brandt21forum.info/bio-graham.html.

"The Camp David Accords After Twenty-Five Years."
Jimmy Carter Library and Museum.
October 24, 2003.
http://www.jimmycarterlibrary.org/documents/
campdavid25/campdavidafter25years.html.

Daw Aung San Suu Kyi. "Message from Daw Aung
San Suu Kyi." Burma Peace Campaign.
World View Rights. March 12, 2003.
http://www.burmapeacecampaign.org.

"Georgia O'Keeffe–The Young Artist."
Ellen's Place. March 26, 2004.
http://ellensplace.net/okeeffe1.html.

"Georgia O'Keeffe." Public Broadcasting Service.
March 26, 2004.
http://www.pbs.org/wnet/americanmasters/
database/okeeffe_g.html.

Goodwin, Doris Kearns. "Franklin D. Roosevelt."
Public Broadcasting Service. May 8, 2003.
http://www.pbs.org/newshour/character/essays/
roosevelt.html.

"Karolyi: I'm Old-Fashioned." ESPN. April 26, 2003.
http://espn.go.com/otl/athlete/karolyi.html.

"Katharine Graham: A Life Remembered."
National Public Radio. March 8, 2005.
http://www.npr.org/news/specials/kgraham/
010717.kgraham.html.

Lewis, Meriwether. "August 17th, 1805 Journal Entry."
Lewis and Clark Trail. January 17, 2003.
http://www.lewisandclarktrail.com.

Marre, Jeremy. "Bob Marley: Rebel Music."
Public Broadcasting Service. March 24, 2003.
http://www.pbs.org/wnet/americanmasters/
database/marley_b_interview.html.

"Martha Graham." Public Broadcasting Service.
November 21, 2004.
http://www.pbs.org/wnet/american
masters/database/graham_m.html.

"New Perspectives on the West: Sacagawea."
Public Broadcasting Service. May 8, 2003.
http://www.pbs.org/weta/thewest/people/s_z/
sacagawea.html.

"1986 Nobel Peace Prize Citation."
Public Broadcasting Service. May 8, 2003.
http://www.pbs.org/eliewiesel/nobel/citation.html.

"100 Greatest Female Athletes." *Sports Illustrated
for Women.* AOL Time Warner Company.
April 26, 2003. http://sportsillustrated.cnn.com/
siforwomen/top_100/9/.

"Online NewsHour: Personal History." Public
Broadcasting Service. February 6, 1997.
http://www.pbs.org/eliewiesel/nobel/
citation.html.

**"Presidential Medal of Freedom Recipient
Katharine Graham."** Medal of Freedom.
June 12, 2005. http://www.medaloffreedom.com/
katherinegraham.html.

"Ruby Bridges–The Interview." Africa Online.
Toonari Corporation. August 8, 2004.
http://www.africanaonline.com/ruby_interview.html.

Schwartz, Larry. "Billie Jean Won for All Women."
ESPN. March 22, 2003.
http://espn.go.com/sportscentury/features/
00016060.html.

Schwartz, Larry. "Michael Jordan Transcends Hoops."
ESPN. September 9, 2005.
http://espn.go.com/sportscentury/features/
00016060.html.

Schweitzer, Albert. "Nobel Lecture: The Problem of
Peace." Nobel Museum. April 22, 2003.
http://www.nobel.se/peace/laureates/1952/
schweitzer-lecture-e.html.

"Sidney Poitier." Public Broadcasting Service.
May 8, 2003.
http://www.pbs.org/wnet/americanmasters/
database/poitier_s.html.

"Women's Voices: Quotations By Women."
About.com. Primedia Company. August 8, 2004.
http://womenshistory.about.com/library/qu/
blqugrak.html.

"Women of the Hall." National Women's Hall of Fame.
Choice One Communications. February 20, 2003.
http://www.greatwomen.org/women.php?action
=viewone&id=95.

WEB SITES

AmeliaEarhart.com
Barbara Haberman ed. CMG Worldwide.
September 18, 2002.
http://www.ameliaearhart.com.

BobMarley.com
Bob Marley Music. March 24, 2003.
http://www.bobmarley.com.

CNN.com
Mitch Gelman. Cable News Network, a Time Warner
Company. August 2, 2004.
http://www.cnn.com.

CNNSI.com
Paul Fichtenbaum. AOL Time Warner.
April 25, 2003. http://sportsillustrated.cnn.com/.

DukeEllington.com
Barbara Haberman ed. CMG Worldwide. August 24, 2002.
http://www.dukeellington.com.

EllaFitzgerald.com
Barbara Haberman and Patrick Howard. The Ella
Fitzgerald Charitable Foundation, CMG Worldwide.
September 18, 2002.
http://www.ellafitzgerald.com.

TheGolfExpert.com
TheGolfExpert.com. March 8, 2005.
http://www.thegolfexpert.com.

Habitat.org
Habitat for Humanity International. March 12, 2003.
http://www.habitat.org/how/millard.html.

HistoryChannel.com
A&E Television Network. April 22, 2003.
http://www.historychannel.com.

Lib.lsu.edu
Mitchell Brown. Louisiana State University Library.
March 8, 2005.
http://www.lib.lsu.edu/hum/mlk/srs216.html.

MarthaGrahamDance.org
Marvin Preston IV Executive Director.
MarthaGrahamDance.org. March 8, 2005.
http://www.marthagrahamdance.org.

NASA.gov
Jim Wilson ed. National Aeronautics and Space
Administration. August 2, 2004. http://www.nasa.gov.

NEA.org
National Education Association. July 18, 2002.
http://www.nea.org

NPR.org
Maria C. Thomas. National Public Radio. January 4, 2002.
http://www.npr.org

NPS.gov
Thomas L. Davies. National Park Service. U.S. Dept.
of the Interior. April 23, 2003. http://www.nps.gov.

O'KeeffeMuseum.org
Jennifer Padilla. The Georgia O'Keeffe Museum.
March 26, 2004. http://www.okeeffemuseum.org.

RFKMemorial.org
Amanda Shanor. The Robert F. Kennedy Memorial.
December 3, 2001. http://www.rfkmemorial.org.

SportsIllustrated.com
Paul Fichtenbaum, ed. Time Warner. March 8, 2005.
http://www.sportsillustrated.com.

uhb.fr/faulkner
The William Faulkner Foundation. July 18, 2002.
http://www.uhb.fr/faulkner/WF/#.

VinceLombardi.com
Barbara Haberman and Melissa Harrold. Estate of
Vince Lombardi, CMG Worldwide. March 24, 2003.
http://www.vincelombardi.com.

Whitehouse.gov
The White House. December 5, 2003.
www.whitehouse.gov.

LECTURES

Aris, Alexander.
Nobel Peace Prize acceptance speech on behalf of Aung
San Suu Kyi. Norway. December 10, 1991.

Edelman, Marian Wright.
"Save the Children." Harvard Medical School
Graduation, Cambridge, MA. February 9, 1997.

Kennedy, John F.
Inaugural Address. Washington, D.C.
January 20, 1961.

Lincoln, Abraham.
Second Inaugural Address. Washington, D.C.
March 4, 1865.

MUSIC

Armstrong, Louis.
Jazz: Definitive Louis. CBS/EPIC/WTG RECORDS.
Audio CD edition, 2000.

Dowd, Tom.
*The Heavyweight Champion: John Coltrane;
The Complete Atlantic Recordings Booklet.*
Rhino Records. April 1995.

Don't Rock My Boat **(Bob Marley)**
© 1972 Fifty Six Hope Road / Odnil Music Limited
(ASCAP). All right for North America controlled by
Fairwood Music USA (ASCAP) on behalf of Blue
Mountain Music, Ltd. And by Fairwood Music, Ltd.
(PRS) for the rest of the word on behalf of Blue
Mountain Music, Ltd.Copyright renewed. All rights
reserved. Used by permission.

Exodus **(Bob Marley)**
© 1977 Fifty Six Hope Road / Odnil Music Limited
(ASCAP). All right for North America controlled by
Fairwood Music USA (ASCAP) on behalf of Blue
Mountain Music, Ltd. And by Fairwood Music, Ltd.
(PRS) for the rest of the word on behalf of Blue
Mountain Music, Ltd. Copyright renewed. All rights
reserved. Used by permission.

Redemption Song **(Bob Marley)**
© 1980 Fifty Six Hope Road / Odnil Music Limited
(ASCAP). All right for North America controlled by
Fairwood Music USA (ASCAP) on behalf of Blue
Mountain Music, Ltd. And by Fairwood Music, Ltd.
(PRS) for the rest of the word on behalf of Blue
Mountain Music, Ltd. Copyright renewed. All rights
reserved. Used by permission.

War! **(Aston Barrett Carleton Barrett)**
© 1976 Fifty Six Hope Road / Odnil Music Limited
(ASCAP). All right for North America controlled by
Fairwood Music USA (ASCAP) on behalf of Blue
Mountain Music, Ltd. And by Fairwood Music, Ltd.
(PRS) for the rest of the word on behalf of Blue
Mountain Music, Ltd. Copyright renewed. All rights
reserved. Used by permission.

TELEVISION

The Genius of Ray Charles. Jeffrey Fager.
60 Minutes. CBS, Boston, 2004.

VIDEO

Legends of Wimbledon: Billie Jean King.
DVD. Standing Room Only, 2005.

Georgia O'Keeffe.
VHS. Home Vision Entertainment, 1993.

Rebel Music: The Bob Marley Story.
DVD. Palm Pictures/Manga Video Release, 2001.

*Frank Lloyd Wright: A Film by Ken Burns and Lynn
Novick.* DVD. PBS Home Video, 1998.

SPEECHES

Wiesel, Elie. "Millenium Lecture Series Speech."
Nobel Lecture. Washington, D.C. April 12, 1999.

Nobel Lectures. Physics 1901-1921.
Elsevier Publishing, 1967.

Chávez, Paul F. "Remarks by Paul F. Chávez."
Unveiling César Chávez Stamp Washington, D.C.
September 18, 2002.

PERIODICALS

—. "J. R. R. Tolkien Dead at 81: Wrote 'The Lord of the Rings.'"
The New York Times. September 3, 1973.

—. "The Crew: Men Apart." Time. July 18, 1969.

Abrams, Irwin. "Aung San Suu Kyi of Burma."
The Nobel Prize Annual 1991. IMG, 1992.

Anonymous. "Building a Movement for All Children."
National Catholic Reporter. June 2001.

Berger, Marilyn. "Katharine Graham of Washington
Post Dies at 84." The New York Times. July 18, 2001.

Church, George. "The Education of Mikhail
Sergeyevich Gorbachev." Time. January 1988.

Colvin, Geoffrey. "What it Takes to Be Great."
Fortune. October 2006.

Edelman, Marian. "There's No Trademark for Kids."
The New York Times. July 29, 2000.

Ewers, Justin. "The Real Lincoln." U.S. News & World
Report. February 2005.

Goodgame, Dan. "The Game Of Risk." Time. August 2000.

Goodwin, Doris Kearns. "Time 100: Leaders and
Revolutionaries: Eleanor Roosevelt." Time. April 1998.

Graham, Martha. "How I Became a Dancer."
Saturday Review. August 1965.

Hall, Ruby Bridges. "The Education of Ruby Nell by
Ruby Bridges Hall." New Orleans, LA.
Guideposts. March 2000.

Hudson, Rev. J. F. "Spiritually Speaking by Rev. J.F.
Hudson." Concord Journal. 2003

Iyer, Pico. "Person of the Year: Corazon Aquino."
Time. January 1987.

Iyer, Pico. "Time 100: Leaders and Revolutionaries:
The Unknown Rebel." Time. April 1998.

Keegan, John. "Time 100: Leaders and Revolutionaries:
Winston Churchill." Time. April 1998.

Kennedy, Edward M. "Eulogy for Robert F. Kennedy."
The New York Times. June 9, 1968.

Kisselgoff, Anna. "Martha Graham Dies at 96;
A Revolutionary in Dance." The New York Times.
April 2, 1991.

Lemonick, Michael. "The Next Giant Leap for Mankind."
Time. July 1989.

Leonard, Jonathan Norton. "Rachel Carson Dies of
Cancer; 'Silent Spring' Author was 56." The New York
Times. April 15, 1964.

Loney, Jim. "Bob Marley (1945-1981)." Otago Daily
Times. May 2001.

McGeary, Johanna. "Person of the Century Runner-
Up: Mohandas Gandhi." Time. January 2000.

Pellegrini, Frank. "Time 100: Scientists and
Thinkers: Albert Einstein." Time. March 1999.

Pooley, Eric. "Mayor of the World." Time.
December 31, 2001.

Rich, Frank. "Don't Follow the Money."
The New York Times. June 12, 2005.

Rushdie, Salman. "Time 100: Leaders and Revolutionaries:
Mohandas Gandhi." Time. April 1998.

Schlesinger Jr., Arthur. "Time 100: Leaders and
Revolutionaries: Franklin Delano Roosevelt." Time.
April 1998.

Schumach, Murray. "Martin Luther King, Jr: Leader of
Millions in Non Violent Drive for Racial Justice."
The New York Times. April 5, 1968.

Smith, J. Y. and Noel Epstein. "Katharine Graham Dies at 84."
The Washington Post. July 18, 2001.

Steffens, Rodger. "The Mysticism of Sound and Music."
The Beat Magazine. April 2000.

Sylvester, George. "What Life Means to Einstein."
Saturday Evening Post. October 26, 1929.

Tannen, Deborah. "Time 100: Artist and Entertainers:
Oprah Winfrey." Time. June 1998.

Thurman, Robert. "A Conversation with Robert Thurman."
Mother Jones. November 1997.

Vancil, Mark. "Michael Jordan: Phenomenon."
Hoop. December 1991.

Wallechinsky, David. "How One Woman Became
the Voice of Her People." Parade. January 1997.

Warrick, Pamela. "A Child's Best Friend."
Los Angeles Times. March 20, 1998.

Williams, Paige. "Vic Braden's Mental Mojo Experience."
New York Times Sports Magazine. November 2006.

photography CREDITS

RACHEL CARSON: Carson at her desk. Courtesy of the Boston Public Library, Print Department.

Page 61 (Part 1, Chapter 6)

UNKNOWN: A Chinese man stands alone to block a line of tanks heading east on Beijing's Cangan Boulevard in Tiananmen Square on June 5, 1989. Courtesy of the Associated Press.

JACKIE ROBINSON: Detail. Jackie Robinson signs a baseball for actor Van Heflin. Courtesy of the Boston Public Library, Print Deptartment.

NEIL ARMSTRONG: Detail. Apollo 11 crew photo. Neil Armstrong, mission commander. 1969. Courtesy of the Johnson Space Center.

Pages 64, 65, 66, 67, 68

UNKNOWN: A Chinese man stands alone to block a line of tanks heading east on Beijing's Cangan Boulevard in Tiananmen Square on June 5, 1989. Courtesy of the Associated Press.

UNKNOWN: Same as above. Courtesy of the Associated Press.

JACKIE ROBINSON: Detail. Jackie Robinson signs a baseball for actor Van Heflin. Courtesy of the Boston Public Library, Print Department.

JACKIE ROBINSON: Courtesy of the Boston Public Library, Print Department.

NEIL ARMSTRONG: Astronaut Neil Armstrong inside the lunar module. July 20, 1969. Courtesy of the Boston Public Library, Print Department.

Page 71

UNKNOWN: A Chinese man stands alone to block a line of tanks heading east on Beijing's Cangan Boulevard in Tiananmen Square on June 5, 1989. Courtesy of the Associated Press.

JACKIE ROBINSON: Jackie Robinson reads the paper. Courtesy of the Boston Public Library, Print Department.

NEIL ARMSTRONG: Neil Armstrong after a mission in the first X-15 rocket plane. 1960. Courtesy of the Johnson Space Center.

Page 73 (Part 1, Chapter 7)

AUNG SAN SUU KYI: Aung San Suu Kyi during an interview at her residence in Rangoon. May 25, 1996. Courtesy of the Associated Press.

NELSON MANDELA: Mandela at his home in Soweto. 1990. Courtesy of the Associated Press.

MOHANDAS "MAHATMA" GANDHI: Courtesy of the Library of Congress.

Pages 76, 78, 80

AUNG SAN SUU KYI: Aung San Suu Kyi waves to a crowd of supporters outside her house in Rangoon. November 26, 1995. Courtesy of the Associated Press.

NELSON MANDELA: Nelson Mandela, at Soweto's Soccer City stadium, near Johannesburg, South Africa, shortly after his release from prison. February 13, 1990. Courtesy of the Associated Press.

MOHANDAS "MAHATMA" GANDHI: Courtesy of the Library of Congress.

Page 83

AUNG SAN SUU KYI: Aung San Suu Kyi during an interview at her residence in Rangoon. May 25, 1996. Courtesy of the Associated Press.

NELSON MANDELA: Courtesy of the National Archives.

MOHANDAS "MAHATMA" GANDHI: Courtesy of the Library of Congress.

Page 85 (Part 1, Chapter 8)

RUBY BRIDGES: Portrait. Six-year-old Ruby Bridges in the doorway of her home. 1960. Courtesy of the Library of Congress.

HARVEY MILK: Harvey Milk in front of his Castro Street camera store. 1977. Photograph Courtesy of Daniel Nicoletta.

ELEANOR ROOSEVELT: Courtesy of the National Archives.

Pages 88, 89, 90, 91, 92

RUBY BRIDGES: Ruby Bridges, guarded by three Deputy U.S. Marshals, enters newly integrated William Frantz school in New Orleans, LA. December 5, 1960. Courtesy of the Associated Press.

RUBY BRIDGES: Ruby Bridges, guarded by three Deputy U.S. Marshals. Courtesy of the Associated Press.

HARVEY MILK: Milk campaigning with longshoremen at the San Francisco Wharf during his bid for the California Assembly. Spring 1976. Photograph Courtesy of Daniel Nicoletta.

HARVEY MILK: Candlelight march in memory of Supervisor Harvey Milk and Mayor George Moscone November, 1980. Photograph Courtesy of Daniel Nicoletta.

ELEANOR ROOSEVELT: Courtesy of the Boston Public Library, Print Department.

Page 95

RUBY BRIDGES: U.S. Deputy Marshals escort six-year-old Ruby Bridges from William Frantz Elementary School in New Orleans, LA. November 1960. Courtesy of the Associated Press.

HARVEY MILK: Candlelight march in memory of Supervisor Harvey Milk and Mayor George Moscone. November 1980. Photograph Courtesy of Daniel Nicoletta.

ELEANOR ROOSEVELT: First Lady Eleanor Roosevelt shakes hands with Pfc. Theodore E. Truesdell at a naval hospital during her tour of the South Pacific in World War II. September 23, 1943. Courtesy of the National Archives.

Page 97 (Part 1, Chapter 9)

WALT DISNEY: Portrait. Courtesy of the *Washington Post*. Reprinted by permission of the DC Library.

BILL GATES: Courtesy of Microsoft Corporation.

KATHARINE GRAHAM: Portrait. Courtesy of the *Washington Post*. Reprinted by permission of the DC Library.

Pages 100, 102, 104

WALT DISNEY: Detail. Walt Disney, center, with member of his staff, and Margie Gay, the star of his *Alice in Cartoonland* series. 1926. Photographer unknown.

BILL GATES: Courtesy of Microsoft Corporation.

KATHARINE GRAHAM: Portrait. Courtesy of the *Washington Post*. Reprinted by permission of the DC Library.

Page 107

WALT DISNEY: Disney describes how he wants balloons to float in *It's a Small World*. 1964. Reproduced from the *Look* magazine photograph collection, Library of Congress.

BILL GATES: Courtesy of Microsoft Corporation.

KATHARINE GRAHAM: Courtesy of the Library of Congress.

Page 109 (Part 1, Chapter 10)

MARIE CURIE: Portrait. Courtesy of the Boston Public Library, Print Department.

ALBERT EINSTEIN: Portrait. Einstein in his home in Princeton, NJ. Courtesy of the Boston Public Library, Print Department.

LOUIS ARMSTRONG: Portrait. Courtesy of the Boston Public Library, Print Department.

Pages 112, 114, 116

MARIE CURIE: Scientist Marie Curie works in a laboratory in this undated photo. Courtesy of the Boston Public Library, Print Department.

ALBERT EINSTEIN: Portrait. 1948. Courtesy of the Canadian National Archives.

LOUIS ARMSTRONG: Courtesy of the Louis Armstrong Archives, Queens College.

Page 119

MARIE CURIE: Scientist Marie Curie works in a laboratory in this undated photo. Courtesy of the Boston Public Library, Print Department.

ALBERT EINSTEIN: Courtesy of the Boston Public Library, Print Department.

LOUIS ARMSTRONG: Portrait. Courtesy of the Louis Armstrong Archives, Queens College.

Page 121 (Part 1, Chapter 11)

TIGER WOODS: Woods at the 2003 Buick Invitational. Februrary 2003. Robert Beck/*Sports Illustrated*.

MICHAEL JORDAN: February 2003. Simon Bruty/*Sports Illustrated*.

NADIA COMANECI: Summer Olympics, 1976. Courtesy of the *Washington Post*. Reprinted by permission of the DC Library.

Pages 124, 126, 128, 129

TIGER WOODS: Tiger Woods at the Masters. October 2004. Robert Beck/*Sports Illustrated*.

MICHAEL JORDAN: October 2004. Bill Smith/*Sports Illustrated*.

NADIA COMANECI: Summer Olympics, 1976. Courtesy of the *Washington Post*. Reprinted by permission of the DC Library.

NADIA COMANECI: Summer Olympics, 1976. Courtesy of the *Washington Post*. Reprinted by permission of the DC Library.

Page 131

TIGER WOODS: Tiger Woods at the Masters. October 2004. Robert Beck/*Sports Illustrated*.

MICHAEL JORDAN: October 1996. Carl Sissac/*Sports Illustrated*.

NADIA COMANECI: Summer Olympics, 1976. Courtesy of the *Washington Post*. Reprinted by permission of the DC Library.

Page 133 (Part 1, Chapter 12)

ANSEL ADAMS: Portrait. Courtesy of the Boston Public Library, Print Department.

GEORGIA O'KEEFFE: Portrait. Courtesy of the *Washington Post*. Reprinted by permission of the DC Library.

MARTHA GRAHAM: Graham with her partner and husband, Erick Hawkins, New York City. May 1950. Courtesy of the Associated Press.

Pages 136, 138, 140

ANSEL ADAMS: Portrait. Courtesy of the Boston Public Library, Print Department.

GEORGIA O'KEEFFE: Portrait. Courtesy of the *Washington Post*. Reprinted by permission of the DC Library.

MARTHA GRAHAM: Portrait. 1948. Courtesy of the Canadian National Archives.

Page 143

ANSEL ADAMS: Portrait. Courtesy of the Boston Public Library, Print Department.

GEORGIA O'KEEFFE: O'Keeffe at 90. Courtesy of the National Archives.

MARTHA GRAHAM: 1932. Courtesy of the Associated Press.

Page 145 (Part 1, Chapter 13)

HELEN KELLER: Portrait. Courtesy of the Boston Public Library, Print Department.

SACAGAWEA: Courtesy of the United States Postal Service.

J. R. R. TOLKIEN: Portrait. Undated photograph. Courtesy of the Library of Congress.

Pages 148, 150, 152

HELEN KELLER: Courtesy of the Boston Public Library, Print Department.

SACAGAWEA: Courtesy of the United States Postal Service.

J. R. R. TOLKIEN: Portrait. Undated photograph. Courtesy of the Library of Congress.

Page 155

HELEN KELLER: Portrait. Courtesy of the Boston Public Library, Print Department.

LEWIS AND CLARK: Painting by Charles M. Russell. Sacagawea, in a boat with Lewis and Clark, meeting a Chinook party. Courtesy of the Amon Carter Museum of Western Art, Fort Worth, Texas.

J. R. R. TOLKIEN: *Lord of the Rings* movie still, Gandalf. Courtesy of New Line Films.

Page 157 (Part 2)

WILLIAM FAULKNER: Portrait. Courtesy of the National Archives.

ROBERT KENNEDY: Kennedy with family. 1966. Reproduced from the *Look* magazine photograph collection, Library of Congress.

LECH WALESA: Workers cheer Walesa, as he leaves the Lenin Shipyards in Gdansk, Poland. June 17, 1983. Courtesy of the Associated Press.

Pages 158, 159

CAMP DAVID PEACE ACCORDS: President Jimmy Carter, Prime Minister Menachem Begin of Israel, and President Anwar Sadat of Egypt. 1978. Courtesy of the Jimmy Carter Library.

Pages 160, 161

DOROTHY DAY: Portrait. 1934. Courtesy of the Library of Congress.

DOROTHY DAY: Courtesy of the *Washington Post*. Reprinted by permission of the DC Library.

Pages 162, 163

MIKHAIL GORBACHEV: Soviet President Gorbachev with his wife, Raisa, talking to reporters in San Francisco, CA. June 1990. Courtesy of the Associated Press.

MIKHAIL GORBACHEV: Former Soviet President Mikhail Gorbachev speaking at Kingsbury Hall at the University of Utah. [in 1991]. October 1996. Courtesy of the Associated Press.

Pages 164, 165

AKIO MORITA: Portrait. Courtesy of the Sony Corporation.

AKIO MORITA: Morita shows first Mavica Video Still Camera and MAVIPACK Magnetic Disk which can record 50 still color pictures. 1981. Courtesy of the Sony Corporation.

Pages 166, 167

RONALD REAGAN: Speaking in front of the Brandenburg Gate in West Berlin, Germany. June 12, 1987. Courtesy of the Associated Press.

BERLIN WALL: A man hammers away at the Berlin Wall as the border barrier between East and West Germany is torn down. Nov. 12, 1989. Courtesy of the Associated Press.

Pages 168, 169

ROBERT AND JOHN F. KENNEDY: Brothers Robert and John standing on the White House portico. 1962. Courtesy of the National Archives.

ROBERT KENNEDY: 1968. Reproduced from the *Look* magazine photograph collection, Library of Congress.

Page 170, 171

GENERAL GEORGE MARSHALL: Portrait. Courtesy of the National Archives.

GENERAL GEORGE MARSHALL: Courtesy of the National Archives.

Pages 172, 173

ELIE WIESEL: Portrait. Courtesy of the *Washington Post*. Reprinted by permission of the DC Library.

ELIE WIESEL: Portrait. Courtesy of the *Washington Post*. Reprinted by permission of the DC Library.

Pages 174, 175

DUKE ELLINGTON: Portrait. Courtesy of the Boston Public Library, Print Department.

DUKE ELLINGTON: Courtesy of the National Archives.

Pages 176, 177

RONALD REAGAN AND CORAZON AQUINO: 1986. Courtesy of the Ronald Reagan Library.

CORAZON AQUINO: Aquino flashes an "L" sign for the word "laban" ("fight") at a rally at Manila's Rizal Park. September 21, 1997. Courtesy of the Associated Press.

Pages 178, 179

WILLIAM FAULKNER: Portrait. Courtesy of the Boston Public Library, Print Department.

WILLIAM FAULKNER: Courtesy of the National Archives.

Pages 180, 181

DALAI LAMA: Portrait. Courtesy of the *Washington Post*. Reprinted by permission of the DC Library.

DALAI LAMA: Portrait. Courtesy of the *Washington Post*. Reprinted by permission of the DC Library.

Pages 182, 183

PELÉ: Courtesy of the National Archives.

PELÉ: Pelé laughs with Special Olympic players. Courtesy of the National Archives.

Pages 184, 185

ELLA FITZGERALD: Courtesy of the Boston Public Library, Print Department.

ELLA FITZGERALD: Ella Fitzgerald: *Caught in the Act* by Art Goldwyn. Courtesy of the Boston Public Library, Print Department.

Pages 186, 187

RUDY GIULIANI: During a ceremony at the Vietnam Veterans Memorial in New York. May 18, 2000. Courtesy of the Associated Press.

Pages 188, 189

AMELIA EARHART: Portrait. Courtesy of the Boston Public Library, Print Department.

AMELIA EARHART: Earhart in Los Angeles after completing her transcontinental flight. 1932. Courtesy of the Library of Congress.

Pages 190, 191

ANWAR SADAT: Sadat and Henry Kissinger. Courtesy of the Library of Congress.

ANWAR SADAT: Courtesy of the *Washington Post*. Reprinted by permission of the DC Library.

Pages 192, 193

LECH WALESA: Workers cheer Walesa as he leaves the Lenin Shipyards in Gdansk, Poland. June 17, 1983. Courtesy of the Associated Press.

LECH WALESA: Courtesy of the National Archives.

Pages 194, 195

MOHANDAS "MAHATMA" GANDHI: Courtesy of the Boston Public Library, Print Department.

MOHANDAS "MAHATMA" GANDHI: Courtesy of the Library of Congress.

Pages 196, 197

SUFFRAGETTES: Courtesy of the Library of Congress.

SUFFRAGETTES: Suffragists picketing in front of the White House. 1917. Courtesy of the Library of Congress.

Pages 198, 199

MICHAEL JORDAN: Jordan during game against the Dallas Mavericks. February 2003. *Simon Bruty/Sports Illustrated.*

Pages 200, 201

SIDNEY POITIER: Portrait. 1959. Courtesy of the Boston Public Library, Print Department.

SIDNEY POITIER: Movie still. Courtesy of the Boston Public Library, Print Department.

Pages 202, 203

VINCE LOMBARDI: Courtesy of the Library of Congress.

VINCE LOMBARDI: Courtesy of the *Washington Post.* Reprinted by permission of the DC Library.

Pages 204, 205

FRANKLIN DELANO ROOSEVELT: FDR and Norman Davis on Amberjack II. 1933. Courtesy of the Franklin Delano Roosevelt Library.

FRANKLIN DELANO ROOSEVELT: 1934. Courtesy of the Franklin Delano Roosevelt Library.

FRANKLIN DELANO ROOSEVELT: Roosevelt holds his Scottie, Fala, while talking to Ruthie Bie, granddaughter of the caretakers of the Hill Top Cottage at his Hyde Park, NY home, in February, 1941. Courtesy of the Franklin Delano Roosevelt Library.

Pages 206, 207

JOHN F. KENNEDY: JFK with wife, Jackie. Courtesy of the National Archives.

JOHN F. KENNEDY: Courtesy of the Library of Congress.

Page 209 (Part 3)

MARTIN LUTHER KING: Dr. King tours Nassau County, NY. May 12, 1965. Courtesy of the Library of Congress.

DUKE ELLINGTON: Courtesy of the Library of Congress.

LECH WELESA: Solidarity supporters carry Walesa outside his home in Gdansk after he was awarded the Nobel Peace Prize. October 1983. Courtesy of the Associated Press.

Page 210

GEORGIA O'KEEFFE: 1979. Courtesy of the *Washington Post.* Reprinted by permission of the DC Library.

CÉSAR CHÁVEZ: Chávez outside the shrine that used to be his car. Delano, CA. 1966. Reproduced from the *Look* magazine photograph collection, Library of Congress.

Pages 212, 213

LOUIS ARMSTRONG: Courtesy of the Louis Armstrong Archives, Queens College.

ELEANOR ROOSEVELT: Roosevelt and United Nations Universal Declaration of Human Rights. 1949. Courtesy of the National Archives.

RACHEL CARSON: Carson, with children, in the woods near her home. Courtesy of the National Archives.

Page 214

AMELIA EARHART: Earhart checking equipment in her airplane. 1937. Courtesy of the Library of Congress.

PELÉ: Pelé laughs with Special Olympic players. Courtesy of the National Archives.

Pages 216, 217

APOLLO MOON SHOT: Closeup of an astronaut's footprint in the lunar soil, taken during the Apollo 11 mission. 1969. Courtesy of the Johnson Space Center.

JOHN F. KENNEDY: Courtesy of the *Washington Post.* Reprinted by permission of the DC Library.

Page 218

ALBERT EINSTEIN: Portrait. Einstein in his home in Princeton, NJ. Courtesy of the Boston Public Library, Print Department.

Back Cover (left to right)

MARTIN LUTHER KING: King hoists five-year-old Martin III in the back yard of their Atlanta home. 1963. Reproduced from the *Look* magazine photograph collection, Library of Congress.

BOB MARLEY: September 1976. Courtesy of the Associated Press.

BILLIE JEAN KING: King in the Wimbledon singles final against Chris Evert. 1973. Courtesy of the National Archives.

MOTHER TERESA: Courtesy of the *Washington Post.* Reprinted by permission of the DC Library.

FRANKLIN DELANO ROOSEVELT: Courtesy of the Boston Public Library, Print Department.

ABRAHAM LINCOLN: Lincoln during Civil War with troops (from left) Scout Adams, Dr. Jonathan Letterman (Army Medical Director), an unidentified person, and standing behind Lincoln, Gen. Henry J. Hunt. Battle of Antietam, MD. October 1862. Courtesy of the Library of Congress.

WINSTON CHURCHILL: Portrait. Courtesy of the Boston Public Library, Print Department.

UNKNOWN: A Chinese man stands alone to block a line of tanks heading east on Beijing's Cangan Boulevard in Tiananmen Square on June 5, 1989. Courtesy of the Associated Press.

CÉSAR CHÁVEZ: Chávez (right) talks with migrant worker outside the shrine that used to be his car. Delano, CA. 1966. Reproduced from the *Look* magazine photograph collection, Library of Congress.

True Gifts™ **Publishing** has made every effort to reach all copyright holders of works featured in this book. If you believe that there are any mistakes or ommisions, please reach us at info@truegifts.net so that we can complete the acknowledgments in subsequent printings.